Making
Precarity
Work

MAKING PRECARITY WORK

Life on the Edge of Venice Beach

LAURA A. ORRICO

The University of Chicago Press
Chicago and London

The University of Chicago Press, Chicago 60637
The University of Chicago Press, Ltd., London
© 2025 by The University of Chicago
All rights reserved. No part of this book may be used or reproduced
in any manner whatsoever without written permission, except in
the case of brief quotations in critical articles and reviews. For more
information, contact the University of Chicago Press, 1427 E. 60th St.,
Chicago, IL 60637.
Published 2025

34 33 32 31 30 29 28 27 26 25   1 2 3 4 5

ISBN-13: 978-0-226-84024-6 (cloth)
ISBN-13: 978-0-226-84026-0 (paper)
ISBN-13: 978-0-226-84025-3 (e-book)
DOI: https://doi.org/10.7208/chicago/9780226840253.001.0001

Library of Congress Cataloging-in-Publication Data

Names: Orrico, Laura A., author.
Title: Making precarity work : life on the edge of Venice Beach /
    Laura A. Orrico.
Description: Chicago : The University of Chicago Press, 2025. | Includes
    bibliographical references and index.
Identifiers: LCCN 2024044761 | ISBN 9780226840246 (cloth) |
    ISBN 9780226840260 (paperback) | ISBN 9780226840253 (ebook)
Subjects: LCSH: Street vendors—Employment—California—Los
    Angeles. | Precarious employment—California—Los Angeles. | Street
    vendors—Government policy—California—Los Angeles. | Job security—
    California—Los Angeles. | Venice Beach Boardwalk (Los Angeles, Calif.)
    | Venice (Los Angeles, Calif.)—Economic conditions. | Venice (Los
    Angeles, Calif.)—Social conditions.
Classification: LCC HF5459.U6 O77 2025 | DDC 381/.180979493—dc23/
    eng/20241119
LC record available at https://lccn.loc.gov/2024044761

Contents

On the Edge

Southern California's beachfront is lined with many pedestrian pathways. None are quite as unique as Los Angeles's Venice boardwalk. Hit by a cacophony of smells, sights, and sounds, visitors find the boardwalk to be a jarring, exciting, and intriguing experience. It is formally known as Ocean Front Walk, and the raised wooden planks one might conjure from its nickname are nowhere to be found. This boardwalk is a mile-and-a-half pedestrian pathway of asphalt and concrete. Its inland side is lined with low-rise buildings and kiosks whose diverse architectural styles serve as a reminder of this neighborhood's colorful past. A few, like the arcade of Windward Plaza and the old Hotel Waldorf stand as proud symbols of Venice's origin as European simulacrum. Others are small retail spaces where merchants roll up their storefront doors to sell jewelry, trinkets, and souvenirs. Restaurants and bars boast small areas of outdoor seating. There is a halfway house where groups of men gather in a front patio, a synagogue whose front door opens onto the pathway, and a cluster of brick shops known as Gingerbread Court that cues some sort of German village.

During my time in Venice, the incoherent architecture felt a fitting backdrop to what could seem like an incoherent social world. Music blared from many directions in an auditorily exhausting competition. Crowds of visitors arrived from around the world to pack the pathway. Young workers in bright-green scrubs emblazoned with a cannabis plant on the back yelled to giggling tourists who passed the entrance of the marijuana dispensary, "The doctor is in! Get legal today!"

By midday, the western edge of the pathway was lined with the vendors, artists, and performers who formed this vibrant public marketplace and iconic attraction. Harry Perry, a turban-wearing electric guitarist, glided by on roller skates, stopping to offer excited tourists a T-shirt printed with his own image. A muscular Black man wearing only a Speedo walked by, smiling in response to stares and more than willing to have his photo taken for a fee. On the grass, a white woman with sunburnt legs lay face down on a yoga mat, likely sleeping off the effects of methamphetamine or oxycodone. Nathan, a classically trained pianist, played Gershwin on his sea-beaten wooden piano. The Wolf Boy walked the five-legged dog from the Freakshow to the grass so it could relieve itself. A man screamed at a barking dog, "I'm not yelling at you, dog! I'm yelling at the turkey!"—which had, in fact, wandered onto the pathway. Joel rolled by on a discarded office chair, trailed by the clatter of empty cans, old dolls, and other odds and ends he had tied to a rope. "I'm bringing bullshit to bullshit!" he yelled. It was hard not to find amusement in the seeming randomness of it all.

But dig a little deeper and one finds that this social world did much more than amuse. And it was anything but random.

I bumped into Emma a half a block from the boardwalk. She had just returned from the social services office in West LA and recounted her experience. She had never wanted to ask for "welfare," she assured me, but she also knew she would not be able to make rent. So, she had gone to the office to request just enough to supplement her earnings for the month—about two hundred dollars. As Emma told me, the women working in the office were baffled by her. "Wouldn't you rather have a real job?" they had asked when she declined job-placement services. But as Emma understood it, any "real" job would be far from a "good" job.[1] It would likely mean working for minimum wage, which she imagined would fall short of supporting her and her son. It would likely mean working without benefits like comprehensive medical insurance, paid leave, or childcare that might otherwise offer some stability for a single mother like her.

Instead, she sold her own artwork on the Venice boardwalk. There she was her own boss. She had the flexibility to see her son off to school in the morning and bring him to work afterward. Plus, she averaged an income she understood to be greater than what she could earn from any 9-to-5. From her perspective, this work was a pragmatic response to precarious conditions. So why was it so hard for those working in the social services office to understand Emma's decision? What might they be missing about the way Emma's life and work came together on the boardwalk? And what might this place offer her that could muddy the seemingly rational choice for a "real" job?

The assumptions of the social service workers echo the prevailing logic that dominates many approaches to urban poverty: namely, that formal employment is key to stabilizing the kind of precarious life conditions Emma experienced.[2] But when we consider the ubiquity of precariousness today—which increasingly defines a large swath of employment and extends into much of our lived experience—such assumptions beg for scrutiny. This scrutiny is only further warranted when we remember that Emma was far from alone in her decision. Each day she joined nearly two hundred other vendors, artists, and performers who also took up this form of informal precarious work, not for what it lacked, but for what it offered.

For some, working on the boardwalk was an opportunity to work with children in tow when there were few options for affordable childcare. For others, it provided an opportunity to make a living with a criminal record in a society that forces people to do much more than their time. Some spoke of it as a way to resist the degradation of low-wage work; some as a way to cope with the injustice of immigration law; others as a way to work despite using drugs and alcohol. Several found an opportunity for work while managing mental health problems.

In this book, I offer a portrait people who live and labor on the edge—the edge of the economy, the edge of legality, the edge of social acceptability, and the edge of the North American continent.

My interests, however, do not lie in documenting how individual participants faced challenges, managed their constraints creatively, and eventually made ends meet. Instead, my interests lie in understanding the boardwalk marketplace as a collective accomplishment, one I found to offer a supportive, though highly imperfect, social system—a system capable of undermining many of the social, economic, and legal systems that otherwise constrained people's ability to meet their own needs. It is understanding how this social system cohered each day, how it gained meaning for people, and with what consequences, that motivates this study.

Urban Poverty, Informality, and Precarity

Many people I met on the boardwalk struggled to gain economic stability. Several were sewing together a patchwork of services to supplement their daily income on the boardwalk, like veteran services, General Relief funds, the Supplemental Nutrition Assistance Program (SNAP), and Temporary Assistance for Needy Families (TANF). Some cycled in and out of jail, particularly as the criminal justice system took up a role in policing issues of homelessness, alcohol and drug dependency, and mental health problems. Other people I got to know were relatively successful in their ability to stay afloat, using income made in the boardwalk's public marketplace to pay rent and car loans and support their families. Some talked about building additional economic opportunities beyond the boardwalk—distributing business cards that directed customers to websites, and traveling to festivals and fairs around the country. The vast majority discussed their participation in the boardwalk's public marketplace as a relatively positive way to navigate life's challenges, even if such narratives ranged from pride to tolerance. Some thought it was the police who should be relieved they had chosen this licit, and public, economy. "It's not like I'm selling drugs!" Marcus said of his choice to sell goods on the boardwalk. Echoing this sentiment, Khaled said to me in acceptance of police surveillance, "At least I'm where they can see me!"

By focusing on the daily impact of broad structural constraints, ethnographic examinations of urban poverty have offered up-close accounts of people who fight for economic survival
through informal means. Building on legacies of housing policy,
segregation, and ghettoization, many urban poor people have
turned to the best economies they can find—licit or illicit.[3] The
drug trade has long served as a source of economic survival for
those left to navigate the effects of deindustrialization and disinvestment, particularly within the Black and Brown communities
left out of postwar real estate opportunities.[4] From the doors and
hallways of dilapidated public housing, poor communities find
themselves "hustling" for survival, adapting to new needs and
opportunities for income.[5] Immigrants dot the urban landscape
as they wait for day labor, sell wholesale goods, and prepare food,
their economic precariousness always compounded by their legal status.[6] Some move about the city as opportunities present
themselves, searching for the kind of "sustaining habitat" that
supports cash-generating activities.[7] Others turn to the material
waste of privileged consumption, salvaging, scrounging, and re-
cycling, since "the vast and concentrated economic inequalities
of city life not only create these material margins, but push the
city's impoverished residents toward them."[8]

With up-close portraits that pay attention to local meanings,
scholars of urban poverty have successfully countered many assumptions imposed on people who strive for economic survival.
Communities so frequently viewed through the lens of disorder
that dominated the late twentieth century construct their own
meanings of decency in the context of limited options.[9] Even
those neighborhoods steeped in illicit economies like the drug
trade create the kind of interaction order that paradoxically pro-
duces and maintains a sense of security and safety residents may
lack elsewhere.[10] Furthermore, scholars have shown that participation in illicit economies is often fed by the very neoliberal
ideology of hard work and private profit that feeds the capitalist
American Dream so valorized around the country.[11]

But dispelling many middle-class assumptions about the urban poor should not work to romanticize such creative adaptations

and strategies. Scholars have also highlighted the strain that poverty places on individuals, communities, and social ties. Poverty can erode trust in the very institutions tasked with alleviating such conditions.[12] Economic niches that rely on an uneven distribution of resources and vulnerability may also allow for greater exploitation.[13] In communities heavily impacted by policing and mass incarceration, people learn to prioritize avoidance of state control over their own well-being.[14]

In this book, many of the cash-generating activities on the boardwalk will resemble other examples of how the urban poor manage to survive. But the Venice boardwalk also defies many common expectations. This social world is not a community of "poor" residents who live in a neighborhood geographically cut off from economic opportunity.[15] In fact, many commute to the boardwalk each day as they might to any other workplace. Neither does this group of vendors fit more familiar portraits of LA's informal economy, where participants are bound by co-ethnicity, histories of migration, and a similar set of social and legal constraints.[16] On the boardwalk, co-ethnic and immigrant networks form a part of a broader social world. People from vastly different backgrounds often sit side by side, communicating in bits of English, French, Spanish, and Korean. In addition, the boardwalk is quite distinct from many portraits of both licit and illicit urban economies, where people recede into the urban shadows to meet their needs.[17] Instead, folks working in the boardwalk's public marketplace remain front and center, on display each day for the tourists who hope to consume their precarious existence as a kind of chaotic carnival. Moreover, this street-level economy does not necessarily emerge to exploit an existing flow of pedestrian traffic but is, in many ways, what *attracts* the pedestrians.[18] Even merchants who were publicly framed in opposition to these non-rent-paying competitors regularly expressed awareness that if the vendors were to leave, so too would their own customers.

Furthermore, while some vendors cling to the few opportunities they have available to them, others have left corporate jobs for the autonomy of entrepreneurialism they find on the boardwalk. The informal sector has offered them access to new and meaningful identities.[19] Narratives of poverty mingle with narratives of self-employment more akin to the creative professionals who populate the nearby coffee shops, begging for better attention to similarities and differences between forms of precarious labor and the "flexibility" these forms may, or may not, engender. On the boardwalk, a geography of poverty meets with an ethic of bohemia, allowing people to reject stigmatized identities and opt (convincingly or not) for other, more celebrated identities.[20] It is difficult to settle on some notion of a "subculture," either as a shared structural position or a common-values orientation. And though it can feel like all are welcome here, it is difficult to celebrate this cultural marketplace as a utopia that suspends privilege and inequality.[21] Instead, the social world here warrants a critical, interactionist approach that allows for attention to tensions, contradictions, and dynamism.[22]

Artists on the boardwalk take different forms, from the formally trained painter to the dumpster-diving sculptor.[23] There are those with mental health issues who cannot find—or who refuse—appropriate care. Some choose the boardwalk to support a lifestyle that is arguably harmful to their physical and mental health. Others find happiness through a form of control over their own future. Such tensions beg for new frameworks capable of teasing apart complex relationships between autonomy and constraint, particularly in an age where precariousness defines most forms of work today, from formal employment to informal day labor.

When, in the late twentieth century, the sociologist Mitchell Duneier examined a group of largely unhoused African American men who sold written matter along Greenwich Village's Sixth Avenue, he was partially motivated to understand the impact of growing poverty as it manifested on the streets of even the wealthiest neighborhoods.[24] In today's economy, the uncertainty and instability we have long associated with poverty now defines a much broader range of experiences. The strategies and practices we associate with managing precariousness are no longer relegated to "the poor." More and more people find themselves having to make ends meet under conditions of ongoing uncertainty, and they are experiencing many of the challenges that shape financial decisions, personal relationships, and a sense of self that come with that precarity.[25] The options available to people as they seek stability seem to have shifted, and as Emma indicated at the start of this chapter, the calculus of weighing those options is far less obvious than we often presume.

For these reasons, I found it difficult to examine this case of urban informality through many common lenses. Urban poverty may have captured the experience of those folks who struggled to make ends meet, but not those successful in securing stable housing, able to support a family and a growing career. It also seemed to dismiss their own self-conceptions, as many would not consider themselves part of the urban poor. A social-problems approach offered some tools to understand those experiencing homelessness, managing harmful drug and alcohol use, and dealing with mental health issues, but it often missed the way people's lived experiences gained meaning each day. The common links between urban informality and immigration, particularly in a city like Los Angeles, encouraged a centering of international migration and legal status, but that captured only one piece of the puzzle. While many people on the boardwalk prided themselves in their artistic talent or entrepreneurial spirit, a focus on creative economies or "flexible" labor belied much of the suffering and constraints people faced. In other words, the boardwalk as a place of urban informality is both typical and exceptional, and it warrants a distinct analytical entry point. To this end, I center precarity as a framework to capture what is happening here.

Scholarship on precarity has grown over the years, often serving as a lens to understand life under conditions of late capitalism and neoliberalism. Having emerged as a political rallying cry in Western Europe, the concept became of academic interest in the early twenty-first century.[26] At times it is broadly equated with uncertainty and vulnerability, though as some have argued, such a sweeping application risks specificity and analytical power. In her overview of the concept, the anthropologist Kathleen Millar highlights three oft-cited works and organizes the concept by its common meanings: as labor condition, class category, and condition of human life.[27]

As a labor condition, precarity emerges as characteristic of the post-Fordist economy and is most often examined through that which it conditions—namely, precarious work. Together with neoliberal policies that valorize the individual as increasingly self-reliant, these "flexible" labor conditions create new subjects who increasingly take on a slew of everyday uncertainties that were once seen as the responsibility of the state.[28] And given the widespread nature of such conditions, precarious work has come to describe a range of activities, from day labor to adjunct teaching.

For some, the flexibilization of work arrangements is lauded as an opportunity for entrepreneurialism, encouraging people to become mini businesses in and of themselves. Individuals are free to follow their "passions," to innovate, to take control of their own economic futures. In this way, precarity is part of a much broader result of neoliberal capitalism, in which people look unto themselves for the means to survive. For others, precarization has its cost. There is more work with fewer guarantees, and the pervasive uncertainty leads many workers to experience negative outcomes.[29] Scholars have warned that precarity as a post-Fordist labor condition isolates and atomizes people, to a degree that they are unlikely to find commonalities, build trust, and forge community. The argument is that the very self-reliance that is characteristic of precarious work only lessens people's political engagement and potential for collective action.[30]

These are the harsh characteristics that led the economist Guy Standing to argue that we are witnessing a new subject position and a new a class in the making—the *precariat*.[31] It is a class category characterized by flexibility and insecurity, left in the wake made by the baby boomers who rode off with their pensions and employment benefits only to change the rules of the game for the next generation.

A different view arises in Judith Butler's focus on the vulnerability of human life and a shared interdependence.[32] This is not, however, to flatten precariousness into a singular shared experience, since, as Millar summarizes, "socio-economic and political institutions distribute the conditions of life unequally."[33] Here, we must be attuned to the distribution of precariousness. There are, in fact, many different configurations of precarity, and the experience of *working* with uncertain hours, fewer fringe benefits, and greater self-reliance will be impacted by one's experience of *living* with insecurity in areas of housing, health, safety, and so on.[34]

Precarity also allows room to understand new modes of living, a possible resistance to the degradation of wage labor, or a refusal of dominant norms.[35] This even echoes some of the original optimism in Keith Hart's use of the term *informal economy*, in which he finds potential in alternative economic arrangements.[36] In this invocation, there is agency and possibility, though as it proliferates in policy spheres, the informal economy becomes increasingly equated with poverty.[37] Precarity, some have argued, may provide a foundation for new political possibilities that reject labor-centered understandings of citizenship.[38] It may act as a space for new possibilities, allowing for alternative relationships between life and work.[39]

I find that the concept of precarity offers a lens capable of respecting many of the tensions found on the boardwalk. It also addresses some of the blind spots that come with prevailing assumptions about poverty and work. It affords an opportunity to recognize different links between precarious work and precarious lives, all of which come with material effects.[40] For instance, the sociologist Waverly Duck used precariousness as a way to understand a local drug economy in terms of communal adaptations to broader structural conditions, an approach that decouples cultural norms from individual values.[41] Kathleen Millar also applied precarity as a lens to examine garbage recyclers on the outskirts of Rio de Janeiro, where she found that people harnessed the potential to create a new form of living. It was not unstable work that destabilizes people's lives, she argued, but rather precarious life conditions that destabilize work.[42]

By approaching everyday experience on the boardwalk through the lens of precarity, I find the room necessary for new relationships between work and life to take shape, free from assumptions about wage labor as a panacea but critical of the precarious circumstances in which people find themselves. Rather than approach precarity as a set of static conditions imposed upon people, this book shows how people collectively negotiate various configurations of precarity.

Inspired by work that prioritizes this relational approach to precarity, this book helps us understand the way precarious life and precarious work come together in everyday experience.[43] First, I argue that people are engaged in a daily practice to *make precarity work*. By this I mean that people organize strategically to manage and capitalize on the shifting regulation of this public space. They navigate, mitigate, and exploit one another's precarious circumstances to make ends meet in the face of inadequate resources and constraints. And they learn to harness and perform a version of precarious living for the public. In other words, people not only transform a set of seemingly unstructured and disorganized practices *into work*, but in many ways, they put precarity *to work*. As the chapters unfold, I show how people produce a workplace from a public space, cultivate a community of workers, incorporate behaviors and experiences often seen as incompatible with work, and generate adaptive skills. While many of the practices of vendors, artists, and performers on the Venice boardwalk are so insecure, informal, and seemingly unstructured that some may fail to recognize them as "work," I find that examining the dynamic ways people make not just money, but meaning, reveals what precarity looks like "on the ground," to those who must navigate it every day.

Next, I assert that we must approach these practices as part of an ongoing and collective production process, one that results in a supportive social system capable of disrupting the social, economic, and legal systems that otherwise constrain people's ability to meet their needs. Workers collectively make private claims over public space and organize socially in ways that undermine the goals of city regulation. They ensure compatibility with people and practices largely excluded from formal employment and controlled through the lens of public disorder. They creatively defy constraints and ensure that the local economy is dynamic, generative, and malleable. In other words, I argue that the practice of making precarity work serves to weave what I call a *subversive social safety net*. And it is a social system that becomes much greater than the sum of its parts.

The subversive social safety net (hereafter shortened to *subversive safety net*) arises, in part, as a response to the inadequacies of the standard social safety net—the array of social provisions and public programs designed to support poor and vulnerable populations. While programs like General Relief funds, Supplemental Nutrition Assistance Program (SNAP), Supplemental Security Income (SSI), and Temporary Assistance for Needy Families (TANF) all offer valuable support for people, decisions about who receives aid, what form aid takes, and which criteria condition eligibility are always shaped by the "moral and symbolic orders" in which they are embedded.[44] In the US, formal employment is the most common condition for access to such programs, thereby drawing stark moral boundaries between the working and nonworking poor as respectively deserving and undeserving. Even for folks who meet such conditions, not only has the rise in neoliberal ideology and policy since the 1980s eroded the reach of the standard safety net, it has stigmatized its use.[45] The subversive safety net blurs the boundaries between work and nonwork, worker and nonworker, deserving and undeserving, and thereby disrupts the moral and legal constructions that condition access to the standard safety net.

But the subversive safety net also takes shape in response to the inadequacies of wage labor—particularly, low-wage labor, or what the sociologist Arne Kalleberg has called "bad jobs."[46] The conditions of such work can be degrading, and employment benefits like paid time off and medical insurance—what has been called the social wage—are increasingly elusive. Without access to comprehensive benefits, people are often unable to meet other life responsibilities. As Emma indicated in the opening scene, a "real" job is not always the stabilizing force others may presume it to be. Instead, she and many other boardwalk participants described turning to such an extreme form of precarious work to exert some semblance of control over a host of life's other insecurities.

The subversive safety net conceptually integrates some key characteristics of the way people met their needs on the boardwalk, including the varied consequences of doing so. First, the subversive safety net is woven through an ongoing dialogue between individuals and the state—including public-space regulation, immigration policy, policing practices, and social service programs. This can and does have the effect of carving out physical, social, and economic space for people to exist, survive, and even locate a dignified opportunity for growth. However, interaction with the state also shapes new forms inequality and vulnerability. For example, the subversive safety net is not exclusive of the federal and state provisions that make up the standard safety net, as Emma indicated in the book's opening when she requested financial assistance to make rent. Instead, people pull from a patchwork of programs and use assistance in innovative and often unintended ways. But rather than support people out of such a precarious situation, they often use bits and pieces of the standard safety net as tools to support their own production of the subversive safety net. They may pay for odd jobs by offering a balance on an Electronic Benefits Transfer (EBT) card or access diagnoses of neurocognitive disorders to gain Supplemental Security Income (SSI).

Second, because this social system is produced by people who experience vastly different configurations of precarity, and because state regulation constantly varies in response to people's daily practices and strategies to disrupt it, social relations are always in flux. Hierarchies are fluid, power dynamics shift, and the kind of sanctions that often reinforce the strict social order of other informal economies are largely ineffective. There is a dynamism to the subversive safety net that gives it robustness and distinguishes it from other cases of urban informality where legal status, physical intimidation, and violence may maintain order.[47]

Third, the subversive safety net allows for key tensions between autonomy and constraint, as well as agency and vulnerability. Any examination of its production requires that we hold multiple realities at once. And the concept itself allows space to recognize both the harmful effects of precarious conditions and the vibrant potential of urban informality.[48]

Finally, while it is a creative and communal response, the social system I describe is also fraught with challenges, exploitation, and suffering. Rather than a laudable accomplishment or a model social world, the subversive safety net can be viewed as a critique of the kind of society that pressures people to produce "work" to meet their needs. The subversive safety net thereby offers a unifying concept that allows us to consider how work and life come together in today's economic, social, and political context, rife with tensions and contradictions. It is a social system that is physically situated, collectively produced, always in production, and inherently dynamic. My hope is that this concept offers a lens that both honors people's humanity and resists unfettered celebration, adding depth and dimension to our understanding of urban informality, urban poverty, and precarious work.

Emplacing Precarity

To understand how the Venice boardwalk came to host such a motley crew, we must examine how the neighborhood became the kind of place where such diverse configurations of precarity intersect. Venice's history gave rise to the kind of ongoing tensions and symbolic slipperiness that makes it difficult to capture through a single lens.[49] Today, some cling to its identity as an amusement playground—a "Coney Island of the Pacific." Some draw pride in its moments of economic decline when it gained fame as a seaside slum and arose from the ashes as a vibrant bohemia. Locals wear the "Dogtown" T-shirts that nod in admiration to the countercultural movement of skateboarding and surfing that emerged in the 1960s and '70s. Others reference the area's fame as Muscle Beach, wearing its emblematic tank tops printed with the image of a bodybuilder. A coffee shop declares "the people's beach" on its wall, reminding visitors that this is no cookie-cutter Santa Monica or Manhattan Beach, but a rare coastal community for those marginalized elsewhere. Self-professed "OGs," or original gangsters, proudly link their identities to the neighborhood's history of gang territory in the 1980s and '90s. Young tech professionals carry canvas tote bags emblazoned with the neighborhood's more recent nickname, "Silicon Beach"—a reference to the boom of service-sector employment and rise of the tech industry in West Los Angeles.

It all began in 1905, when "Venice of America" opened as the realization of a millionaire's dream. Having amassed wealth through the tobacco industry, Abbot Kinney acquired the undeveloped marshland with the vision to transform it into a playground for visitors, replete with the canals, gondolas, and arcaded architecture of its Italian namesake. Many of those visitors arrived via Pacific Electric's Venice Short Line, part of Los Angeles's impressive mass transit system that carried riders from downtown to the coast. There they were delighted by an array of amusements, including bikini contests, exotic-dancing shows, strongman demonstrations, musical performances, a fun house, and piers that extended the entertainment over the ocean.[50] People packed the beaches and crowded the attractions. And, as the growing motion-picture industry used the area as a setting for films, it solidified Venice as a must-see attraction for decades.

But in November 1920, Abbot Kinney died, and only weeks later, the amusement pier was destroyed in a fire. The loss of the pier, difficulty with infrastructure maintenance, and ongoing sewage issues on the beach turned the tide on what had previously been staunch opposition by "Venetians" to the prospect of joining the city of Los Angeles. The growing number of year-round residents voted for annexation, and in 1925, Venice became another neighborhood in the growing metropolis. Many hoped the decision would bring greater funds from the city to support Venice's unique character, but local and national trends pulled LA, and consequently Venice, in a somewhat different direction.

Decentralized growth had sowed the seeds for Los Angeles's idiosyncratic love affair with the single-family home and the single-occupancy vehicle—a love affair at odds with Kinney's Venetian creation.[51] Though the pier itself was rebuilt, the waterways and streetcar lanes that had defined the neighborhood were unable to accommodate the rise in automobile usage. As a result, the city decided to fill in many of the canals. In addition, economic decline in 1929 meant fewer tourists with expendable income for entertainment. Though the area continued to attract visitors, Venice's economy remained afloat with profits from oil and growth in the defense industry.

Aircraft manufacturing, such as the Douglas Aircraft Company, had moved into neighboring Santa Monica in 1921 and continued to be a major employer in the area. Many workers found housing in nearby Venice, including an African American community that settled in a small tract known as Oakwood. The community was a vestige of Kinney's need for labor, and he had permitted African Americans to settle in the area away from the canal zone. In fact, when Kinney willed his own house to his chauffeur and assistant Irving Tabor, Tabor was required to physically relocate the house to Oakwood in order to avoid the racially restrictive covenants that excluded him from occupying it in its original location. In what remains a relatively rare nonwhite coastal community to-day, Oakwood continued to attract Black families for decades.[52]

War was a boon to the economy during the next decades, and from 1945 through the 1960s, in Los Angeles as well as the rest of the country, there was a rise in the manufacturing, construction, and transportation industries. In what came to be known as the Fordist era, the American economy was marked by standardization of production processes and suburbanization-fueled consumption patterns. With a rather secure contract between labor and capital, the country saw a rise in full-time jobs, decent wages, strong labor unions, and new opportunities for training and advancement.[53] A supportive sociopolitical system initiated through President Franklin D. Roosevelt's New Deal programs worked to harness and restrict market forces and provide additional stability in the form of social security, unemployment, housing loans, and education support.[54]

But many of the New Deal policies that preceded and followed the war would also draw deep divisions of race and class in the American landscape. Social security benefits had excluded agricultural and domestic workers—positions held largely by nonwhites. The new low-interest, long-term mortgages that had sparked suburbanization were approved through a racist appraisal system that viewed nonwhite communities and racial mixing as negative financial investments. As a result, roughly 98 percent of the funds available to subsidize homeownership through mortgage loans went to white families, granting them disproportionate access to wealth-building equity and the quality education and resources that come from a robust tax base.[55] And while public housing had federal support, funds were made available through a voluntary application system; few white suburbs applied.[56] Across the country, many Black and Latino communities were relegated to urban areas vulnerable to disinvestment, laying the foundation for what would become the American "inner city."

While Los Angeles's decentralized form complicated stark distinctions between "suburb" and "urban core," investment and disinvestment patterns still resulted in a patchwork of neighborhoods with an uneven distribution of resources.[57] In Venice, when the Kinney company's lease on the pier ran out in 1946, the city of Los Angeles chose not to renew it. Much of the pier was either dismantled or destroyed, and amusement facilities moved north to Santa Monica. Echoing narratives of urban decline around the country, the writer Lawrence Lipton called Venice a "slum by the sea."[58] But rather than apply such a label with disdain, Lipton was one of many who had come to Venice precisely because they were drawn to the remnants of urban America.

With lower rents than surrounding neighborhoods and a history that set Venice apart from the more conservative lifestyle of the rest of Los Angeles, the 1950s brought a countercultural group of artists and writers that would become known as the Beat generation. The Beats rejected the standardization of labor under Fordism and the conformity of suburban living, and instead sought the seeming "authenticity" of the very communities that had been excluded from New Deal programs. The Beats settled alongside the "nonwhite populations, homosexuals, drug addicts, and outlaws" who aligned with their own urban aesthetic.[59] In Venice, as other bohemian districts in New York City's East Village and San Francisco's North Beach, the state of urban decay offered a setting ripe with the possibility to live an alternative lifestyle to that of such a sterile rational world.[60]

In the following decades, the beatniks were joined by "hippies" and "flower children" who railed against the mass production and consumption of a postwar Fordist economy, infusing Venice with their antiwar, feminist movement and ushering in the kind of cultural marketplace we still find today. The area also established its reputation as a site for roller-skating, acrobatics, bodybuilding, and fitness. Soon, Muscle Beach became a tourist destination and attraction, again serving as a prime setting for the film industry.

In the late 1960s and '70s, the pier just north of Venice that had previously been known as Pacific Ocean Park sat rotting along the coast. Yet, once again, a group of young people saw potential in the remnants. The dangerous infrastructure became the site of a daring surf culture, where teens proved their skills by navigating the remains of the pier. A group of surfers turned skateboarders soon found new ways to engage with additional parts of the dilapidated landscape around Venice and southern Santa Monica, including skateboarding in local pools left empty by drought.[61] As a result of these innovations, the area gained the nickname "Dogtown"—the nickname still professed with pride today. What had been a playground for wealthy and middle-class visitors in the early 1900s, had become known for its grit. And with the glitz and glamour of Santa Monica to the north and the newly dedicated harbor development of Marina del Rey to the south, Venice seemed a world apart.

The nature of opportunity in Venice continued to shift alongside changes in the global economy. Immigration policy in 1965 and the movement of global capital sparked new immigration patterns, and during the latter half of the twentieth century, Los Angeles transformed from among the whitest metropolises in the country to its most racially and ethnically diverse. In the 1980s, the proportion of Latinos in the city grew by 71 percent, and the next decade it again grew by about 40 percent, increasing the Latino population from 400,000 to 2.8 million.[62] Such demographic shifts manifested in Venice, as a growing Latino community formed in the once African American section of Oakwood.[63]

In those same decades, the Asian immigrant population grew from around 75,000 to 1.1 million.[64] Korean immigrants began to open small businesses around the city, including small shops along the inland side of the Venice boardwalk.[65]

But post-1965 immigrants had entered an economy far different from those of prior generations, and even though Los Angeles's manufacturing industry remained relatively robust, it still mirrored national and global economic trends. Production had turned toward a global market, bolstered by new communication technologies. By the mid-1970s, the world experienced a globalization of products, capital, and labor markets. Public-sector employment decreased; many of the jobs that had served as boons to the American middle class evaporated as firms sought low-wage production rates abroad to satisfy the needs of institutional investors rather than workers. By the end of the 1980s, a record number of Angelenos had filed claims for jobless benefits.[66] Manufacturing waned and Los Angeles more than doubled its employment in service-sector industries. By the 1990s, about 40 percent of all employment was in service-sector jobs.[67]

As the Fordist era had been marked by a supportive sociopolitical system, the new focus on "flexible" labor was accompanied by the retreat of the government in its role to harness the forces of the market. With the presidency of Richard Nixon, the country set off in a full embrace of neoliberal policies that shifted power and control to the private sector. The federal government increasingly rejected responsibility for economic security and anti-poverty programs, shifting the burden to lower tiers of government. While some states attempted to fill the needs of its residents, others passed the federal reductions to clients, thus resulting in a reduction in funding for health, housing, income, human services, and community development.[68] Women, African Americans, and Latinos were increasingly participating in part-time employment and low-wage industries; as a result, they became particularly vulnerable. The loss of job security was now coupled with an inability to acquire quality health care and adequate housing. Both labor *and* life were increasingly characterized by precariousness.

In California, the loss of federal support for the healthcare system in the 1980s resulted in one of the country's worst records for health services to the poor. Federal funding for housing programs declined, sparking a crisis of affordable housing that soon became a crisis of homelessness. Deinstitutionalization and a lack of funding for mental health programs left many people dealing with mental health problems without proper care.[69] Treatment programs for drug use declined precisely at the time the country saw a rise in crack cocaine use and addiction.

In Los Angeles and across the country, the precarious life conditions resulting from national and global trends began to manifest on city streets, and under neoliberal ideology, such life conditions were more often viewed through the lens of individual behavior than societal issues. By the end of the twentieth century, visible poverty, street-level economic activity, homelessness, mental health problems, and drug use were viewed as a type of "disorder." A turn toward the containment of social issues, and people's attempts to navigate them, meant a rise in policing and a growing reliance on the criminal justice system in lieu of treatment or economic support. Both drug offenders and those dealing with mental health issues increased as a proportion of a rapidly growing inmate population. By 1991, the LA County jail was operating as the largest psychiatric institution in the nation.[70]

Seeking economic opportunity in the new economy, an increasing number of people turned to LA's streets and public parks to make ends meet. Street-level economic activity dovetailed with immigration patterns shaped by globalization; the same shift during the 1980s to police "disorder" led to a more exclusionary approach to public spaces. Clashes between vendors, residents, and merchants further fueled quality-of-life policing and poverty-management strategies that created what the geographer Don Mitchell has called a "brutal public sphere."[71] Across the country, cities began passing sidewalk ordinances to limit the uses of sidewalks. Los Angeles responded to a resurgence of street vending with one of the most stringent vending ordinances in the country.[72]

With its history of bohemian and countercultural communities, Venice had laid the groundwork for a somewhat supportive approach, even developing something akin to what the sociologist Mitchell Duneier has called a "sustaining habitat."[73] Social service agencies worked to fill gaps in care. In the late 1980s, the St. Joseph Center expanded from a small volunteer organization to a nonprofit organization capable of serving the growing homeless population. The organization adopted a slightly different approach than that of downtown's Skid Row, where policing often ushered poor residents into religious missions.[74] At least in mission, the St. Joseph Center built on Venice's history and focused on the autonomy of individuals. Meanwhile, the Venice Family Clinic served the healthcare needs of many who found themselves otherwise without care. The boardwalk itself served as a frequent site for food distribution to those in need, with organizations like Food Not Bombs regularly distributing meals.

Meeting new requirements from the California Coastal Commission, founded in 1972, parking restrictions were also more lenient than in other neighborhoods. Though not without conflict, this supported some vehicular living—a form of shelter that plays a major role in housing people in the area today. And as vehicular homelessness continued to grow across the city, people became vulnerable to any shifting parking restrictions that limit access to the street.[75]

In Venice, local politicians similarly sought to control the growing economic activity along the boardwalk. Many argued that the boardwalk's economy had turned from a venue for artistic expression in the 1960s to a commercial marketplace for the downtrodden. In the 1980s and '90s, the city initiated and continued to revise a local ordinance, Los Angeles Municipal Code 42.15, to distinguish "commercial vending" from "free speech" activities, issuing tickets to participants selling commercial objects. In doing so, they created a formal designation for the boardwalk as a "Free Speech Zone." As the sociologist Andrew Deener has noted, such parameters did not necessarily create more restrictions, but rather paved the way for a growing number of low-income participants to "adapt, challenge, and revise the law."[76]

And such an economic opportunity gains even greater significance when considered in the context of LA's highly restrictive
public-vending laws.[77]

Vending restrictions continued to play out alongside a growing
income divide, which was even starker in California than the rest
of the US, and starker still in Los Angeles. Reaping massive benefits from the state's booming service economy, billionaires tripled
in number in the 1990s. At the same time, the median household
income fell and the number of people in poverty increased.[78] By
the turn of the twenty-first century, about 20 percent of Los Angeles residents lived in poverty, up from 13 percent a couple of decades earlier.[79] Poor and nonwhite neighborhoods concentrated in
the center and south of the city, with the most destitute in downtown's Skid Row, while high-income areas persisted along the
western coast and in the foothills.[80] The divides were geographically distributed and patterned along racial and ethnic lines.

Following urban unrest around the country and in South
Los Angeles in particular, Venice would also become the center
of attention for violence and bring the area's racial fissures to
the fore. Between 1993 and 1994, fifteen African American and
Latino residents died in what was labeled a Venice "gang war."
More than fifty others were injured. The ongoing violence had begun at a public housing project in the Mar Vista neighborhood
a few miles inland of Venice and soon shifted to Oakwood (the
historically Black neighborhood where, a century prior, Abbot
Kinney had encouraged African American workers to settle). Now
wedged between the white wealth of Santa Monica and Marina
del Rey, local gangs had identified an economic niche in the illicit
drug trade. Three self-proclaimed "gangs" now vied for control:
the Shoreline Crips, a largely African American group; and the
Venice 13 and the Culver City Boys, both largely Latino. The violence received extensive media coverage that framed the tension
as a geographically situated racial conflict, announcing: "Deadly
Venice Gang War Turns to Race War."[81] However, more-complex
analyses show that in framing the event as a "race war," the media overlooked other shifting cleavages.[82] Still, the Oakwood area
of Venice had historically been "L.A.'s most visible black locale

along the coast."[83] Venice, shaped by new immigration patterns, economic inequality, and a rise in the drug trade, was portrayed in the media as deadly and dangerous—both of which were undeniably racialized.

The divide between the haves and the have-nots only grew as the twentieth century came to a close. Venice and Santa Monica each saw increasing homelessness on their city streets and their public parks, while the area's quirky bohemian identity also attracted many high-paying service-sector jobs. As the sociologist Richard Lloyd has argued, high earners in the service sector often draw on a bohemian ethic of contingency and vulnerability to adapt successfully to the precarious work arrangements of the new economy. Furthermore, it is for this very reason that enterprises eager to exploit such qualities have gravitated to these bohemian neighborhoods.[84]

Venice is no exception. In a nod to the tech boom of Northern California's Silicon Valley, the area was dubbed "Silicon Beach" by the early 2000s. Creatives in the tech industry settled along Los Angeles's west side; in 2011, Venice solidified its central role when Google moved its LA headquarters a couple of blocks inland from the boardwalk. Embracing Venice's quirkiness to its fullest, Google took up residence in a Frank Gerry-designed "binocular building" that had previously housed an advertising firm. It also moved new offices adjacent to the famous Gold's Gym, a site of Venice's remaining bodybuilding culture. And in a rather clear illustration of the economic and social trends of the time, the padlocked door to those Google offices opened directly into a growing community of unhoused people who found residence in tents, temporary structures, and vehicles.

On the boardwalk itself, the tech startup Snapchat moved into a former marijuana dispensary. With only an image of a cartoon ghost displayed, the former Stanford twentysomethings played Ping-Pong on the patio, giving the building more the appearance of a spring break venue than an office building. The company's boardwalk beginnings, however, ended with one of the largest IPOs in LA history, and their physical footprint grew to take up nearly 305,000 square feet of office space in the neighborhood—offices that then brought private security to the area.[85] Both Google and Snapchat served as major indicators of the neighborhood's rise in tech, but they also became the frequent focus of ire from longtime participants in the boardwalk's economy. "Ever since Google moved in . . ." became the prelude to many a complaint about commercialization, policing, and a loss of Venice's character.

Wealth has continued to pour into the area. The small canal zone that was renovated in the 1990s and its picturesque waterways and arch bridges are now home to a rather exclusive and affluent community. And though Venice adopted a slower growth model than did neighboring areas, its quaint residential streets are lined with small yet increasingly luxurious bungalows. Some multimillion-dollar fortresses hide behind manicured hedges. Creative professionals crowd into small-batch coffee shops. The boardwalk itself has welcomed hip new restaurants and bars replete with glass enclosures and cabana-like seating. Charming "walk streets" are lined with homes whose wooden gates hide behind overgrown gardenia and bougainvillea bushes. At the same time, much of Venice's population remains "on the edge." Those quaint residential walk streets terminate at Speedway, the pothole-ridden alley littered with overflowing trash bins, discarded mattresses, used needles, and the remains of disassembled bicycles. Homelessness continues to grow—a reality made starkly visibly in 2020, when, following the global health crisis, the unhoused population in Venice increased by 50 percent and encampments dominated the beachfront scenery.[86]

Today, such historic developments allow Venice to take on different meanings for different people. It is at once a wealthy playground, a seaside slum, Dogtown, "the people's beach," gang territory, a coastal Black enclave, "Silicon Beach," and so much more. It is this multifaceted and frequently "contested" history that allows Venice to be experienced and harnessed in distinct ways.[87] People latch onto different narratives and symbolic meanings to make sense of their participation in the boardwalk economy as a part of their life trajectory. In other words, the history of this place imbues people's lives and activities with meaning by allowing them to link their narrative and their role in the local economy to one or more of the neighborhood's identities.

When the sociologist Forrest Stuart examined everyday life in downtown LA's Skid Row, he met a man grappling with the significance of being there. Skid Row is a place notoriously known as the homeless capital of America; with a population around 70-75 percent Black, it is a stark illustration of racialized abject poverty. The "territorial stigma" of Skid Row meant that the man's mere arrival as a Black person himself served as a wake-up call. He told Stuart that upon finding himself in Skid Row, he knew he had hit "rock bottom."[88] Conversely, when I spoke with Khaled, a Black vendor on the boardwalk who was also unhoused and struggling to make ends meet, he had a very different framing of his presence in Venice. As we spoke about policing and new regulations, Khaled sat back in his chair, put his feet up on the table from which he sold goods, and proudly declared, "They just don't want to see a Black man at the beach with his feet up."

It is the complex history of Venice vis-à-vis the city's and the country's own sociopolitical history that allows Khaled to frame his daily work not through the lens of lack and loss, but as a form of resistance. He is Black. He is at the beach. And the soles of his shoes act (albeit temporarily) as a middle finger to state control. As we will see throughout this book, the many tensions that arise from global, national, and local forces often mingle together on the boardwalk in unexpected ways as the subversive safety net reveals itself to be a complex social world capable of supporting vastly distinct configurations of precarity.

The Ethnography

I lived in Venice for five years while I completed my PhD in sociology at UCLA. During that time, I observed, assisted, and worked alongside participants in the boardwalk's public marketplace. I did not move to Venice with the specific goal of performing research; rather, I found that my academic interest in public-space usage dovetailed with my desire to live in a neighborhood with a vibrant public life. With only a bike and a bus pass to take me to and from campus, my version of Los Angeles was, to a large extent, Venice.

Over the course of five years, my time on the boardwalk varied alongside my additional commitments. There were months I could spend most days on the boardwalk, collecting data from early-morning hours into evenings. There were months during which my ongoing role as a teaching assistant limited my available hours, though my residence in the neighborhood meant I always returned to check in with people and witness both stability and change. Even on days I boarded the Big Blue Bus to campus, I consistently purchased my morning coffee at Groundwork, the tiny coffee shop just off the boardwalk. As an active person, I regularly ran and biked along the boardwalk; I was a member of the famous Gold's Gym; I frequented neighborhood restaurants, bars, and cafés; and I attended town halls and meetings of the Venice Neighborhood Council.

During my observations and participation, I typically jotted notes into a small notebook and returned home in the evening to type up more detailed accounts. On occasion, I used a recording device, though only for formal interviews and public meetings. Most of my observations and conversations took place while I sat with participants. However, in 2013, I began to establish myself first as an assistant to one vendor and then as an artist myself, selling prints of watercolors I painted. I was initially reluctant to work independently, since it meant isolating myself in a single space; but I was surprised how much my independent work proved a vital component of data collection. The experience affirmed many of the processes I had witnessed over the years, and also provided new details of daily practices that emerged only as I navigated my own participation in the marketplace.

Following my graduation from UCLA in 2015, I moved two hours inland for a postdoctoral fellowship. Though no longer immersed in the daily life of the boardwalk, I was able to return for frequent visits. After moving to Philadelphia for work in 2016, I returned to the boardwalk for brief but informative visits in the summers of 2019 and 2022.

Trained in an interactionist tradition that values meaning-making processes, I applied an abductive analysis that encouraged movement between surprising findings and literature.[89] My focus therefore shifted over time as I sought tensions and puzzles within this social world. I began the project by getting to know various vendors, artists, and performers who worked along the boardwalk, and had some initial instincts that conflicts over city regulation would be a central focus of the project. But like many ethnographers before me, I found my initial instincts were limited. City regulation was just one piece of a much larger story.

A major strength of ethnography lies in its capacity to follow processes over time, allowing what may seem like catastrophic ruptures in social life to smooth into ebbs and flows. I became interested in the ongoing and collective construction of stability under what seemed like uncertain and atomizing conditions. I sought analyses that paid respect to the tensions of everyday life on the boardwalk—tensions through which the boardwalk's social world cohered in rather surprising ways. As a result, I remained dissatisfied with defining the boardwalk's marketplace through a single lens. The people and practices I witnessed did not fall into clear typologies. My natural tendency to relish life's gray areas was both professionally and personally challenging, but I hope, in the end, worthwhile.

I have tried to make my own presence visible to the reader throughout this book, since I never sought nor found it plausible to be a "fly on the wall." There were days when I laughed and enjoyed the company of people I met, naively trying to make "good" decisions about where to draw boundaries. Inevitably wrapped up in the complex relationships and histories of people working here, my experience had highs and lows. There were days when I feared for my safety. There were moments, be them all fleeting, when I considered leaving academia to be a street artist. There were afternoons I'd return to my apartment to sit on the floor in the dark, trying in vain to calm myself after the constant hum of energy and unrelenting sun of daily work on the boardwalk.

Though my focus in this book remains on the situated practices of work, I also traveled "beyond" the boardwalk. I attended public meetings of the Venice Neighborhood Council, and I served on two neighborhood council subcommittees: the Boardwalk Task Force and the Health and Safety Committee. The former subcommittee formed in the wake of a temporary injunction to the city ordinance that regulated the boardwalk. We met in the public meeting space of a storage facility to brainstorm revisions to the ordinance and submit suggestions to the Venice Neighborhood Council, none of which ever made it into the revisions. The Health and Safety Committee formed following the death of a young woman from Italy who was traveling on her honeymoon. She was struck by a vehicle while walking with her husband; the car that struck her had swerved around the concrete bollards in place to block vehicular traffic and was purportedly driven by a man having a mental health crisis. This group was led by local first responders, and our meetings often centered on finding small implementable solutions to massive social issues, like erecting plastic bollards and decorative bike racks to block cars—but not emergency vehicles—from reaching the pathway, and placing large garbage cans in the parking lots so people could store blankets and, hopefully, slow a recent outbreak of scabies.

At times, I visited people in their homes, whether houses, apartments, or vehicles. I witnessed the various nooks and crannies that people occupied, somewhat surprised by the shelter available in what was otherwise some of the most coveted real estate in LA. I traveled with vendors to downtown Los Angeles as they purchased merchandise for resale, learning more about the way the local economy spread beyond the confines of Venice. Such ongoing proximity to people was, again, both fruitful and rife with challenges.

My being a young single woman in my early to mid-thirties undoubtedly shaped my general access to data, the kind of data I accessed, and the lens I applied during analysis. Unmarried and without children, I was sometimes taken as a friendly ear, a potential romantic partner, a liability, or a public companion. Much like the ethnographers I read during my graduate training, I sought out people able to act as "informants" or key research participants who might guide me toward important lines of inquiry, introduce me to new sources, and help me learn more about the context of life here. As I have written about before, such an approach at times led to greater access, but also moments of constraint.[90]

Though I do not want to overstate any commonalities, my place in the social world of the boardwalk may defy some common assumptions. My living arrangement was not unlike several vendors I met. Over the course of five years, I first sublet a studio apartment on the boardwalk, then shared a small bungalow two blocks inland, and finally rented another studio apartment half a block from the boardwalk. That said, being a graduate student at UCLA with a cushion of financial support from my family gave me a level of security and career aspirations distinct from many other participants on the boardwalk. My ability to spend money at local bars and restaurants somewhat set me apart as well, though it was not unusual to run into vendors and artists at nearby establishments—when I went to the Venice Ale House just off the boardwalk, I ran into Hazel enjoying some beers with friends; Ricardo regularly invited me out to join him and his friends for salsa dancing at bars in Marina del Rey and Santa Monica.

In addition, vendors and artists lived in each of the buildings where I rented studio apartments. In the first studio I rented, I lived upstairs from Tim, a man who was recently divorced, working as a vendor, and receiving unemployment benefits. In true Venetian fashion, the building felt more like a college dorm than a formal apartment building, and I often visited Tim downstairs and witnessed the rotating group of people he invited in for a shower or place to sleep. Another apartment building consisted of three floors of three-hundred-square-foot apartments and a communal library in the entrance. There, I lived across the hall from Rachel, a trained artist who had sold her paintings on the boardwalk for a time but had since shifted away from the marketplace for other endeavors. I frequently visited her apartment, occasionally attended yoga classes with her, and offered some support with childcare for her then infants.

In Venice, differing social positions did not lead to the kind of stark segregation one might expect in other urban areas. The live-in landlord of my apartment building frequently spent time with Emma, the artist from the beginning of this chapter. Kurt, who had been unhoused, befriended one of the building owners nearby and became a regular in-house artist, even working on local murals. Some vendors would meet up for backyard barbecues in the neighborhood. Artists and residents, whether housed or unhoused, mingled in the coffee shop each morning.

My racial and ethnic background, as the daughter of a Puerto Rican mother and an Italian American father, offered me a somewhat malleable identity. With dark curly hair and olive skin, I tended to register as somewhat racially and ethnically ambiguous, particularly in the context of Los Angeles race relations. Even though I identify as Latina, I almost never cued Mexican or Central American origin, which were more common Latino identities in LA. Far more often, I was taken as mixed race: part Black, part white, or maybe Brazilian, maybe Israeli—somebody "not-quite-white" but also "could be white." Many Black Caribbean and African American workers discussed race and racism quite freely with me, though considering I taught on topics of race and racism, I do not want to imply that such conversations flowed only because of some sense of shared identity. My ability to speak Spanish afforded me greater access to a large immigrant population on the boardwalk, and as a result, I was often privy to more informal conversations and jokes exchanged between Spanish-speaking friend groups. I was also able to communicate with new arrivals from around Latin America, some of whom did not speak English.

While it is always difficult to know how one's identity becomes salient in the varied interactions that take place during research, I believe the most notable aspect of my racial and ethnic identity was that it quickly and frequently emerged as a point of curiosity, up for discussion. It was also malleable enough that a diverse set of people found parts of my identity to which they could relate. At times, the boardwalk could seem like a place where strict lines along racial, class, and gender identities held little purchase.

But daily interactions often illuminated the fissures that percolated beneath the surface. For example, one day following an argument with a Black vendor, I walked to sit with a group of Latino men and began speaking Spanish. When the vendor walked by, he invoked a social and racial boundary, yelling, "This is where you belonged all along!" When Randy, a self-proclaimed activist, got fed up with the large immigrant networks that procured some advantage in finding a space from which to work, he yelled, "The INS really needs to come!" When a white man named Anthony found himself assisting a Black vendor, he started hurling racist epithets at the vendor. He said he was angry at the perceived injustice of being a white man working for a Black man. When a resident saw me at the coffee shop, he looked down at my feet and proclaimed, "Oh, I didn't see your flip-flops!" Having thought I was barefoot, he laughed and said, "I thought you'd gone native"—implying a boundary between myself and those more truly "on the boardwalk." When I got embroiled in some "drama" by failing to offer the kind of companionship one male vendor desired, a female vendor worried that being seen with me could increase her own vulnerability; she asked to separate from me as we approached the boardwalk, noting, "They're always watching."

Navigating the boardwalk's social world was tricky. I do not set aside specific sections of this text for social constructs like gender, race, and class, mainly because they could not be set aside in everyday interaction. Nor do I want the stories that follow to romanticize my experience. It was often the trickiness of navigating social relations that led me to discover important mechanisms and meanings. Like many social worlds replete with people who shared deep histories filled with love, friendship, betrayal, and forgiveness, at times the boardwalk felt like a minefield of what those working here called "drama." No amount of access, time, or relationship building could have allowed me to fully overcome that challenge, because it was and is a part of this complex social world.

In the presentation of my own data, I have used pseudonyms for the people working on the boardwalk. In cases where I reference a person with a public identity, I have used their public name. I have also represented the dialogue in a way that respects the language people used in the setting, as I always noted specific phrasing in my notebook, since it illustrates important local meanings.

Chapter Outline

In what follows, I outline an up-close account of people managing precarity through a daily practice of *making precarity work*. When taken together, such practices weave a supportive social world that disrupts the dominant sociospatial order, resulting in what I call a *subversive safety net*. To begin, chapter 2, "Producing a Workplace," examines the way people navigated and negotiated the city's regulation of public space to access—and consequently produce—a workplace. I spotlight the final months of a permit program that was initiated to eliminate the perceived monopolization and competition of the prior first-come-first-served policy. This chapter follows people as they organized socially around the permit program to ensure that the space served as a reliable workplace. I show how people created new patterns of interaction, forged employment relationships, and developed an aftermarket exchange for parcels of public space. They engaged in both formal and informal claims-making strategies, even filing a lawsuit that eventually led to an injunction of the ordinance. Chapter 2 therefore illustrates how making precarity work entails not only navigating regulation, but actively shaping the conditions that structure economic opportunity. By the end of the chapter, we gain an understanding of how people undermined the city's conception of this public space to assert their own. The first strand of the subversive safety net comes into focus: a workplace from which to earn income.

Chapter 3 moves to an additional part of the process to make precarity work—cultivating a community of workers. To understand the everyday ways people in the boardwalk economy built and defined this vital community, I examine trust as a key social mechanism. I document the way people built, maintained, and protected trust in ways that mitigated ongoing uncertainty and produced long-term economic stability. I follow interactions and exchanges that ranged from the simple and immediate task of watching over belongings to more time-intensive and consequential interactions like protecting one another from external threats. By following these interactions as they were built over time, I illuminate an additional strand of the subversive safety net: a robust community of workers capable of mitigating the uncertainties endemic to informal precarious work.

In chapter 4, "Incorporating the Undesirable," I show how experiences intertwined with precariousness are included in this social system. I focus attention on visible and prevalent substance-use practices—practices that also become bound up with experiences of homelessness and mental health issues. I argue that the tendency to focus on abject abuse and disorder—particularly when analyzing the drinking and drug use of marginalized groups in urban America—has left a blind spot in our understanding of how substance use gains meaning in people's lives and how urban economies can become experienced as complicated sites of support. Rather than approaching people as patients and clients, the chapter approaches them as economic and social actors. By decentering abuse, I expose variations in how people integrated their substance use with work, how substance use became tied to people's understanding and organization of time, their roles and identities, their relationships, and their vulnerability to surveillance and law enforcement. In the end, this process exposes yet another strand of the subversive safety net, as a social system capable of incorporating practices (and people) often seen as undesirable and incompatible with work.

In chapter 5, the final substantive chapter, I show how people make precarity work by making a sale, which on the boardwalk was far more extensive than a simple economic exchange and entailed navigating the physical, legal, and social conditions of the marketplace. Though such skills are often overlooked in this form of labor, chapter 5 shows how people built their knowledge from which to make decisions about what, when, and how to sell their goods and merchandise. With no overarching management, no contracts, and no official data on consumer demand or competition, people still gathered the data necessary to make important decisions. They weighed the cost of gas against the prospect for income. They were forced to consider the risks of competition when sharing the secrets of their success. And they found themselves working within the constraints of a local ordinance that regulated which activities and merchandise were permissible in this Free Speech Zone. What we find is that the boardwalk marketplace was not a venue for public expression but rather a dynamic and generative social world in which people could learn to participate. This generative capacity thus becomes another strand of the subversive safety net: the chance to gain adaptive skills, affording an opportunity for people to become expressionists.

The concluding chapter summarizes the main assertion of the book, that what results from these daily practices to make precarity work is a *subversive safety net*. I summarize the key characteristics of this safety net and build on prior scholarship of informal support systems. While a "safety net" may work to support people at any given moment, I also assert the need for a critical lens. As any safety net, there is ongoing inequality and marginalization. Many of the practices involved in making precarity work reproduce the very precarious conditions people are attempting to overcome. In addition, the very notion that people must produce "work" is deserving of our criticism and reflection regarding labor-centered notions of citizenship and access to basic resources. Finally, I move beyond the case of Venice Beach to show how the framework of a subversive safety net may offer a unifying lens with which to understand the ways precarious life and labor come together.

Producing a Workplace

"These guys will kill you over that piece of sand!" Kenny announced. "Tully is scum—the scum of the earth!" he told me of another musician with whom he had just had an argument. Kenny said he had played guitar on the boardwalk since the '70s, when, as he put it, "there was really nobody." A white man with scraggly blond hair, his classic Venetian style hovered somewhere between naturally disheveled and curated cool. Visibly pissed off, he told me, "We all fight for these spots. We're like crabs in a bucket!"

Unlike Kenny's state of agitation, it was a peaceful and cool Tuesday morning. The Pacific Ocean shone a bright blue in the distance; a picturesque warning of the hot July sun soon to envelop us. Kenny and I were gathered with around three hundred other people outside of the modern brick Venice Beach Recreation Center and Police Substation just west of the boardwalk, all of us waiting for the weekly lottery draw to determine who would access space from which to sell goods, artwork, and perform.

Quite distinctly, Kenny's anger conveyed nothing of the passive process of waiting. Instead, he equated finding space with a deadly competition. His comments were even more puzzling since the lottery draw that we awaited that day was precisely the city's effort to quash any fighting over spots. As one of many forms of public-space regulation on the boardwalk, it was part of the Public Expression Participant Permit Program, designed to end the long-running first-come-first-served approach the city believed had limited access to "only the strongest and earliest arrivals." The lottery, by contrast, operated through a random drawing, designed to ensure the fair and equitable distribution of parcels of concrete from which people could earn income along the boardwalk.

But the discrepancy between Kenny's definition of the situation and that of the city's reveals a much larger discrepancy in their conception of public-space usage. Randomized chance might be fine for folks who entertained a hobby here and there, but it was far from acceptable for people who relied on this public space for their livelihood.

In this chapter, I begin to show how people in the boardwalk economy made precarity work by collectively navigating and shaping city regulation. As they did, they carved out the social, economic, and physical space from which to earn income. This involved far more than erecting the physical infrastructure that visitors witnessed at the 9 a.m. start time. Like many marketplaces, the boardwalk was a daily social accomplishment, and this accomplishment involved producing (and reproducing) a set of economic roles, personal relationships, and claims-making strategies.[1] I argue that this collective practice to make precarity work served to transform the open concrete into a daily workplace, and as a result, it wove an initial strand of the subversive safety net. It established a viable and vital workplace that undermined the city's conception of appropriate public-space usage, confused the boundaries between work and nonwork, and disrupted many legal and social barriers to work.

Empirically, I focus attention on one period of city regulation: the Public Expression Participant Permit Program. It was one of the more heavy-handed attempts to control access to the marketplace, but it was just one of many attempts to regulate access to the marketplace. However, public-space regulation often provided a shifting set of rules in this workplace—rules that people must resist, navigate, and harness to meet their needs.[2] As is evidenced throughout this book, the rules of the game continued to change, contributing to the dynamic nature of the subversive safety net.

Over the course of five years, I witnessed a few changes to regulation of the boardwalk, and I also heard impassioned stories about regulation prior to my arrival. And while public space is always regulated at multiple levels, Venice's participants—as well as merchants, property owners, and residents—were most concerned with major and minor revisions to Los Angeles Municipal Code 42.15. It was 42.15 that defined and regulated the boardwalk's Free Speech Zone through various approaches like the permit program. In fact, when I asked people about their experience on the boardwalk, 42.15 was almost always a key part of their narrative.

When I began research, it was such narratives that led me to believe any change to LAMC 42.15 would be immensely impactful. And changes did, of course, have an impact. But the benefit of long-term ethnographic research is that it affords primacy to processes over time. As years passed, I came to see that ongoing shifts in regulation represented dynamic waves of change, but rarely caused severe ruptures to the social and economic life of the boardwalk. Regulation played only one role in the ongoing tension between autonomy and constraint. As we will see, the subversive safety net becomes robust by remaining dynamic and responsive to change. And as a social system, it takes on a character somewhat distinct from common examples of informality where hierarchies and power dynamics are rather stark and static, protected in ways that are highly consequential.[3] The subversive safety net shifts form as the practices to make precarity work adapt to the constraints and opportunities of state and local regulation and policing practices. The result is a system where power dynamics are in flux and hierarchies change.

The Permit Program

For decades, the Venice Beach boardwalk marketplace offered space for artists, performers, and other expressionists to access the multitude of visitors who passed through each year. People accessed space on a first-come-first-served basis and set up their goods in the amount of space they required. But the kind of broader social changes that led to widespread precarity, both in the US and globally, also touched down on the boardwalk. In a city that otherwise banned public vending, competition for space increased. In the 1990s, Los Angeles began regulating the space more formally, leading to the creation of what became known as the Free Speech Zone alongside a bevy of "time, place, and manner" restrictions. Concern arose that the first-come-first-served policy had sparked a problematic monopolization of space and physical intimidation, even if evidence of physical fights was limited.[4] To address concerns, however, the city imposed a program designed to afford interested participants a greater chance of access, essentially allowing a more egalitarian distribution of spaces. What emerged in 2005 was the Public Expression Participant Permit Program, an approach to public-space usage vehemently opposed by many longtime participants for its attempt to restrict one's First Amendment right to public expression. The program took months to get off the ground, lasted for five years, and ended abruptly when a lawsuit filed by participants themselves was successful in deeming it void for vagueness (though the shorthand on the boardwalk was that it had been found "unconstitutional").

During the years the program was in place, however, the mile-and-a-half pathway was divided into 205 "designated spaces." Each measured roughly twelve feet by ten feet and was defined by painted borders with a number at the center. The linear pathway was further divided into different zones, I and P, which carried subtle distinctions in permissible goods and activities. Participants were then required to make a onetime twenty-five-dollar purchase of a plastic ID card—inaptly representative of a "permit." The spaces themselves were distributed to permit holders through a weekly lottery draw held on Tuesday mornings. The draw ran throughout the entire year for the I zone and during summer months for the P zone. There was also a separate draw for weekday access.

In addition to managing the distribution of designated spaces, the permit program imposed additional "time, place, and manner" restrictions that impacted access in peculiar ways. Amplified sound was widely banned, except for a few clusters of adjacent spaces. Expressive materials like books and pamphlets were permitted, as well as items "inextricably intertwined with a political, philosophical, religious or ideological" message. To appease opposition from longtime expressionists who believed any restrictions over access violated their First Amendment rights, there were opportunities to participate without a permit. There were spaces designated for food distribution. A few "black" spaces free from any permit requirement were accessible on a first-come-first-served basis. Plus, at noon, unoccupied spaces became fair game, regardless of participation in the program. However, if the person who had rightfully "won" the space in the lottery returned at any point later in the day, they could claim the space for themselves.

If all this sounds confusing, it is because it was. And without third-party management or formal agreement of participation, many of these rules were either gleaned from posted signage on the pathway or—more frequently—informally communicated between participants themselves.

This rather complex application of public-space regulation should not be confused with any meaningful "formalization" of economic activities. Unlike more common manifestations of permitting processes, participants did not go through any official registration process; their credentials as artists and expressionists were never reviewed, identities never verified, and addresses never collected. Many people submitted false names, and quite a few participants did not have any permanent home address. The ID cards themselves offered no guarantees to space or pay. And while the program was administered by the Department of Recreation and Parks, infractions were largely enforced by the Los Angeles Police Department (LAPD), making the permit program one more arm of state control over public-space usage.

The program was therefore confusing and fraught with conflict. Many people who had been participating in the boardwalk marketplace prior to the permit program could not shake the fact that they were now being asked to pay twenty-five dollars for the *chance* to access public space. And, to add insult to injury, this public space had become known as a Free Speech Zone to allow

First Amendment-protected vending. It was this fact that often bubbled up in the ongoing opposition between many longtime participants—who felt that access should result from time and effort exerted—and the city—which sought to ensure a system that paid no homage to seniority or intimidation. Watching how it played out, however, tells us something important about the way power dynamics emerged on the boardwalk, how they shaped different forms of success, and how they led to shifting social hierarchies and exploitation.

The Lottery Draw

Each Tuesday morning, a diverse crowd gathered around the recreation center and police substation. Hopeful participants ranged from age eighteen to eighty, Black, white, Latino, Asian, Middle Eastern, Eastern European. Some were dressed in the slacks and blouses of business-casual office attire. Others wore faded jeans and colorful tie-dye prints, their clothes splattered with paint. A few men sat in canvas folding chairs reading the *Los Angeles Times* while they waited. Some leaned against carts and wagons, filled with the blankets and sleeping bags that likely had covered them in the street the night before. Skateboards, bikes, and rollerblades lay scattered on the grass. Small children roamed around the jungle gym. A woman sold tamales from a handheld basket. Every now and again a surfer cut through the crowd—feet bare, board tucked at their side. An onlooker would have been hard pressed to locate any coherence to the crowd, and yet here we all were, waiting for the weekly lottery draw to determine who would access the space from which to earn an income.

The lottery required participants to hand their individual ID card to a representative from the Department of Recreation and Parks. The representative threw the cards into a rotating bingo cage that sat atop a couple of folding tables. At the start of the draw, he would turn the handle, mix up the plastic cards, and pluck them out in groups of five. Those five names were then announced to the crowd, and the five lucky "winners" would form a line.

The 205 available spaces, however, fell far short of accommodating the number of interested participants. Since the boardwalk's informal economy presented a rare opportunity to earn licit income in a city that had an otherwise strict ban on public vending, it drew quite a few people who wanted to work. And for many of the people seeking to sell goods and services, it was not a weekend hobby but a matter of livelihood. The competition for space left a rather harsh paradox between the apparent whimsy of the lottery draw and the severe hardship that could result from lacking space for work. Consequently, the public event was rife with drama, conflict, and humor.

"Julian Denton! Mr. Peppa Peppa! Don't Nobody Know My Name! Carissa Reynolds!" One by one, the names were called. Lacking any kind of formal registration process, many of the names listed on ID cards were chosen for their entertainment value—a way for resentful vendors to participate in the lottery system while also resisting its perceived infringement on their right to space. This was, in many ways, an everyday act of resistance.[5]

"I won! I won!" Julian jumped up with his arms outstretched in the air. He smiled and laughed. Julian, a Latino man who had grown up in Venice, spent years as the resident drummer on the boardwalk. Now in his forties, he lived in an RV that he parked on the street. Energetic and friendly, Julian loved to poke fun at the absurdity of the lottery draw by playing up the idea that people could *win* access to public space. Absurdity aside, he was happy; he would be able to perform and earn some cash for the upcoming week.

Julian jogged over to the station, his thick brown hair bouncing by his shoulders, and he joined four other lucky participants to form a line in front of the folding table. One by one they stepped forward, signing their names in a book next to a number that corresponded with the "designated space" they would occupy temporarily. In return, they received a blue raffle ticket that served as a tangible, albeit flimsy, claim to their parcel of public space.

While the process may seem straightforward, few people simply threw their single ID card into the bingo cage and waited for the chance to be called. Instead, "playing the lottery" was informed and shaped by the practice of making precarity work; most participants were resigned not to leave their participation up to chance. As a result, the program sparked new strategies to exert control over access to income-generating activities, thereby undermining the purported goals of city regulation. It sparked new ways of socially organizing, imbued the concrete with new "value," and created new social hierarchies and power dynamics.

Navigating the Program

Partnering and Pairing

Jay came over and asked if I'd like to join Hazel and him in the lottery. With the peak season about to start, Tim had already asked me to join RJ and him in the lottery as well. My inclination was to remain neutral, and so I declined. Along with many of the participants in the marketplace, Jay and Tim were scrambling to put together a small group that could increase their odds of accessing a designated space. The logic was simple: If your ID card was chosen in the lottery draw, you could pick a space and take a ticket. If it wasn't, you were out of luck. It didn't take long for people to realize that the more ID cards, the greater the chance of "winning." But people couldn't simply purchase multiple ID cards, as one might do with lottery tickets, and they couldn't borrow ID cards either. Since participation in the marketplace was founded on "individual expression," the logic assumed one person per space. ID cards had to be attached to individual people, and those people had to be physically present at the Tuesday lottery draw. It didn't take long for folks to realize that access had become a numbers game.

I first met Tim while he was selling a set of random merchandise on the boardwalk. A tall, thin white man in his thirties, Tim was always full of big ideas. He was going to expand his business. He was going to run for city council. He was going to fight the bus lanes in Westwood and homelessness in Venice. Each time he had a new idea, he explained it with overflowing energy and the full swing of an imaginary baseball bat. Tim's story was both commonplace and anomalous—commonplace because he was at a juncture in his life, just off a divorce and out of a job; anomalous because he received unemployment benefits and owned a condo in a wealthy neighborhood of Los Angeles that his brother currently occupied.[6] In the meantime, he rented a small studio just off the boardwalk.

During the lottery, Tim played the numbers game by turning to the readily available homeless population on the boardwalk. Most consistently he turned to RJ, a white man in his forties who was originally from New Jersey, with a background in construction. RJ had seen his fair share of hard times. "I didn't use to be the oldest," he told me in reference to the death of his five siblings, "but now I'm the oldest." As a result, he took care of his mother until she was eighty-six; then he left. "I lost my tools, apartment, truck, and got on a plane with seven dollars," he said, rolling right past the gaping holes in his personal history. When he landed, he needed some place to go, he told me. He had heard of Venice Beach, so he came here. He started sleeping on the street, selling goods for people here and there, running errands and doing odd jobs. It was an all-too-familiar story of rupture, loss, and heading west with few resources.

In the years I knew RJ, he was always kind, though serious and often disgruntled from drinking too much or not drinking enough. He rented part of a storage unit where he kept some belongings, and he slept in a parking lot a mile from the boardwalk. Each day he rode his bike from the lot, many times freshly showered from a nearby shelter and towing a cart neatly packed with the belongings he needed to get through the day. With the lottery, Tim saw an opportunity in RJ to "help the homeless," and arguably himself, while RJ saw an opportunity for some startup capital. Tim paid for RJ's ID card and merchandise and agreed that RJ could work within the same space for a commission—about a dollar on every five sold. This way, if either was chosen, both would have the opportunity to work.

Tim and RJ represent a common way participants navigated the permit program, and they illustrate some of its varying effects.

For one, the permit program socially and economically linked homelessness to the boardwalk landscape in more formalized ways. In some cases, the partnerships provided an opportunity for people to earn income and eventually invest in merchandise of their own. More often, the arrangements were vastly unequal, as Tim not only supplied the financial capital and transportation to purchase new merchandise, but often dangled resources in front of RJ like food, a place to sleep, and access to a shower. Precisely because Tim could meet some of RJ's needs in exchange for his added ID card, this relationship vacillated between supportive and exploitative.

"*I* was supposed to do the hematite!" RJ yelled one morning. He had been selling this jewelry for a few months by that time—a set of necklaces and bracelets made from a gray mineral believed to have curative properties. "He got into my market!" Though anger over competition was rare in the marketplace (a point I return to in chapter 5), RJ and Tim were physically sharing a table. RJ had thought there was an informal agreement of support—or at least not direct undercutting—and RJ had begun to think of himself as establishing his own business focused on selling hematite jewelry. But when Tim saw the hematite selling, he also bought the jewelry and began selling it. Now the two were in a competition rather skewed in Tim's favor.

Tim and RJ's partnership went through phases of growth and decline. There were the months when Ángel and Russel, both artists just "passing through," joined up with the group. The two new men were traveling independently and sleeping wherever they could each night. They painted during the day and sold items on Tim's table, occasionally using his apartment for showers and a place to crash. There were the months that Tim and RJ joined together with Jorge and Rennie, two unhoused men engaged in rather heavy alcohol use. Jorge frequently set up another artist's goods. Occasionally women would appear, like Adriana, to whom Tim took a liking; he hoped sharing a table would blossom into something romantic. In a couple cases it appeared to work out, albeit briefly, and in other cases, such as with Adriana, Tim just ended up frustrated.

This is one of many ways power dynamics on the boardwalk were shaped by people's distinct configurations of precarity. But while this form of partnering and pairing was a rather unstructured way of banding together to increase the odds of earning income, some other participants took the numbers game even further. For those able to draw on large kinship and co-ethnic networks, there was an opportunity to establish more structured and hierarchical employment relationships.

Building an Operation

Co-ethnic groups became particularly visible at the lottery draw. West African immigrants often congregated, wearing red, green, and yellow clothing known as "Rasta wear," some with wooden carvings of the African continent around their necks. Latino men, along with some women and children, sat on the concrete wall by the jungle gym, most originally from Mexico and Central America. The characteristics of immigrant networks, where co-ethnics ranged from the well established and documented to the newly arrived and undocumented, often fit the opportunity structure of informal work arrangements like street vending.[7] Many such networks fared well under the lottery system, turning the public space into a viable workplace for people whose immigration status acted as a barrier to formal employment. For those with some capital, co-ethnic networks became an asset in the construction of a scalable business or, as was the going phrase on the boardwalk, building an "operation."

I met Matías in the spring of 2010. Originally from Colombia, Matías had lived in California most of his life. He worked only the most lucrative days: Thursday through Sunday. He was one of the participants who preferred the lottery and complained that the first-come-first-served era required him to come very early in the morning to reserve a spot. At least this way, if you were chosen, you knew you had a spot, he would tell me.

Over time, however, I could see that Matías had other reasons to like the lottery. Matías sold relatively high-quality jewelry, much of it designed with large turquoise and jade stones. He displayed necklaces on small busts, setting his merchandise apart from jewelry displayed flat on a table. Matías told me this was his main job, and that he himself made the jewelry. I have many reasons to doubt this, particularly since his own employees stated otherwise, but it was the story Matías told.

One morning before the 9 o'clock setup time, I walked up to Matías to say hello. He was preparing to work across from Farid's jewelry store on the inland side of the boardwalk, which Farid himself often lamented for the competition. Matías introduced me to a man standing next to him, telling him in Spanish that I was doing some research on the boardwalk. "Juan," the man said while extending his hand and continuing to chat with me in Spanish. Juan had recently arrived from Medellín, Colombia, and told me he did not speak much English. Tall, slim, and in his twenties, Juan looked like he had just stepped out of a nightclub. He frequently sat working on a small laptop, his hair neatly gelled, a fresh shirt with the collar popped, a few buttons open to reveal his chest. He was working with Matías and had received a spot down the boardwalk through the lottery; he'd be selling Matías's merchandise.

Juan was one of several men from Colombia who began to work with Matías—or more accurately, working for Matías. Juan told me he was a carpenter by trade, but since he was "not legal," he was having difficulty securing employment. Juan said if he wanted to get his business off the ground, he could sell Matías's jewelry for a small commission.

Lacking proper documentation for employment was a rather frequent motivation for earning income through these networks. Emilio, a gregarious man in his thirties with a cherubic round face and a big smile, also told me he "lacked papers." Like Juan, he had arrived in the US from Colombia and began working with Matías while he waited for more regular employment. Emilio understood his participation in the boardwalk economy as a temporary gig, though he did not seem in a hurry to change this arrangement. After all, Matías provided merchandise for Emilio to sell, and Emilio earned a commission. Different from Juan, however, Emilio had also secured a place to live with help from the network. He rented a spot in a studio apartment with a few other Colombian men. Though small, the studio was well organized, with a kitchenette and an open floor that fit multiple mattresses on which the men could sleep. Most important, it was located adjacent to the boardwalk.

"Matías makes a lot of money," Juan told me as we sat waiting for the lottery draw to begin. "More than most people," he added. Juan believed Matías's success had a lot to do with his economic capital, telling me that Matías had the money to invest in higher-quality products from downtown. But he also believed Matías had a good knack for sales, since he paid attention to the kind of jewelry people liked. As we sat there on that Tuesday morning, Matías had clearly increased his odds of earning income by hiring several men to work for commission. Matías himself would claim one of the spots and those in his network would claim any additional. "He's got a bunch of people working with him now," Juan explained, telling me that at least four of the men had ID cards tumbling around the cage that morning.

These employment networks relied on one person, like Matías, with enough financial capital to invest in multiple ID cards and merchandise, and a steady stream of people who lacked such capital, like Juan and Emilio. For some of these men, the employment relationship proved useful. For instance, Emilio eventually secured a more permanent position in New Jersey and made the trip east to work. However, it wasn't long before he returned. Juan eventually secured some construction work in the San Fernando Valley, though he too reappeared for some quick cash here and there.

Their network was not unique. Ousmane helped a fellow Senegalese immigrant get started with some Rasta wear until the guy earned enough to begin purchasing his own merchandise. After "bottoming out" (typically a reference to losing all one's resources because of alcohol or drugs), Raúl arrived on the boardwalk and joined a group of Mexican immigrants who sold the goods of one other man, their "*primo*," or cousin. These larger networks were quite hierarchical, but they also satisfied many of the participants' immediate needs. Significantly, this way of socially organizing disrupted the lottery system's "egalitarian" distribution and merely shifted the power from "the strong" to "the well networked."

Both the process of partnering and the process building an operation in the boardwalk economy were shaped by the precarious life conditions of those involved, as well as the uneven distribution of resources that granted some more social and economic capital than others. Specifically, these operations were shaped by current immigration policy and an uneven distribution of global capital. When work relationships took shape in this context, it was not uncommon for forms of exploitation to develop alongside opportunity.[8] Furthermore, the hierarchies that resulted were also precarious. After all, in just a couple of years, jewelry would be banned on the boardwalk, and Matías would not fare so well under the new regulation. It was just one more way the subversive safety net comprised dynamic power relations, as it was in constant dialogue with shifting state regulation. And it was another way the power dynamics of the subversive safety net were distinct from the more static social networks that define other cases of urban informality.

Amplifying the Weekly Upheaval

The permit program developed from the city's belief that access should be an even playing field. But the same strategy to limit monopolization by the few acted as a spatial and social upheaval. That constant reorganization sparked the need to negotiate shifting power dynamics anew each week. This was particularly acute among musicians, precisely because they experienced the greatest spatial constraints. In fact, the distribution of "amplified" spaces—those spaces exempt from the ban on amplified sound—was quite illogical. Their case indicates the complex processes that people in the boardwalk marketplace used to attempt to disrupt the city's regulation of space and reproduce a valuable workplace.

Kenny, who in the opening to this chapter was livid as he told me about the competition over spaces, was a musician on the boardwalk; so were Reggie, Tully, Peter, Julian, Brian, and Gerald. A mix of white, Black, and Latino men, musicians had a particularly competitive experience in the context of the permit program, specifically because the city imposed the permit program and lottery alongside restrictions on amplified sound. These restrictions had a chaotic effect on musicians when vying for a spot in the lottery. Musicians still had to join forces in order to increase their chances of performing (and earning tips) for the day. And yet, the numbers game looked quite different when we consider a major issue: musical performances cannot occur concurrently on adjacent spaces—at least, not if one expects an audience to shell out tips for the performance. So, having three "amplified" spaces next to one another did not translate into three simultaneous performances.

In addition, since amplified musicians relied on tips, they often preferred to play for a stationary crowd who could listen to an entire set. They also relied heavily on the businesses along the east side of the boardwalk, particularly restaurants, developing a very clear hierarchy of numbered spaces in relation to them. "Nineteen is perfect!" Reggie told me, referring to a space directly across from the outdoor seating area of a popular restaurant. What we find is a small window of space deemed appropriate by musicians, and it was an issue they had to resolve anew each week.

While the musicians formed some partnerships, the majority existed as components of a band: guitarist, drummer, bassist, singer, pianist, and so on. Each individual musician held their own ID card for the lottery draw, and depending on who was able to secure one of these desired spots, the entire group was thrown into a negotiation over how to arrange a band, how to rotate sets, and who gets priority over others. The social relations of musicians arose out of these very particular spatial restrictions. And as a result, they had to produce a workplace within a workplace.

I sat with Peter at the draw one Tuesday morning and commented that the atmosphere seemed quite enjoyable. People come to the event with very different needs and goals, and it struck me as an opportunity for them to gather. While tourists may see a bustling social space, working alone in a designated space could feel isolating

and lonely, and the lottery draw was a stark contrast to the typical workday. As we sat at the lottery together, people told jokes and
reminisced about the old days.

"Everybody is friendly on Tuesdays," Peter told me. But then
he explained the fragility of such camaraderie: "Until they call
the names out, there's nothing to fight over." He laughed. "Nobody knows whose ass to kiss yet."

It was a simple statement, yet one that described a significant
outcome of the lottery system. While it thwarted intimidation
and monopolization, it also forced people to address the shifting
hierarchies and power dynamics that came with either holding or
lacking a ticket. For musicians, figuring out "whose ass to kiss"
was a weekly process. And the tone could change in an instant.
We saw in the opening to this chapter that it was during the lottery when Kenny emphatically assured me, "These guys will kill
you over that piece of sand!"

Though no such sanctions ever came to pass, some musicians
did have it easier than others. For instance, Julian was one of only
a few drummers and was generally welcome to play with a variety of other musicians. Guitarists and vocalists were in a rougher
position, as Paul often noted. Too many people seemed to "think
they have guitar skills," he told me, leaving guitarists to scramble
for a spot along the boardwalk.

Different from many formalized performance spaces, the
boardwalk did not screen people for talent. For instance, when a
woman who often sang with recorded musical accompaniment
was one of the first participants called in the lottery, other musicians must deal with the likelihood that she would choose a prime
space. "Karaoke this weekend! Karaoke time!" Kenny yelled as
an insult. When the woman received her ticket for the weekend,
she grabbed her skateboard. As she turned toward the hill where
the musicians gathered, she looked up with a smile and yelled
back, "Haters!" While the interaction hovered between frustration, anger, and light comedy, it also illustrates that the egalitarian distribution of spaces offered yet another layer of debate over
"deservedness."

Under the permit program, the musicians never comfortably settled on a stable system; they rarely avoided conflict. But they also kept complete monopolization at bay. When Julian came over to tell me he was tired from playing with everybody, he added that he had to "deal with" Peter and Kenny getting into a physical fight. "And it's my spot!" he yelled. But Julian, as a drummer, needed companions to play as a group. In the case of the musicians, the lottery distribution of the space did nothing to quell the conflict over access.

Finding New Ways to "Work" the Market

Pierre returned from getting his lottery ticket for the weekend and rejoined a group of us sitting on a concrete ledge. Not more than a second after he sat down, he jerked his torso back as if struck by something. "I forgot I'm not even going to be here this weekend!" he said. He leaned forward and rested his forearms on his knees, seeming to settle into the news. Then he said calmly, "I can probably get fifty for the weekend."

It was not uncommon to sell a space. And upon hearing Pierre's comment, the group launched into a debate about whether it would be a "good weekend" or not. After all, fifty bucks was top dollar. They discussed weather predictions, time of year, and weekend events, since this was the mix of important variables that could predict the potential for customers and, consequently, the value of the spot.

As the permit program and lottery system reverberated through the social world of the boardwalk, not only did it spark new ways of understanding ownership over public concrete, new ways of forming relationships, new sets of winners and losers, and new conflicts, but it also gave birth to an entirely new market for spaces and a new way to think about a day's work. In essence, the permit program and lottery system had constructed an exchangeable commodity in the designated space, and thus introduced a new strategy to make precarity work: to extract income from the space itself.

The practice of selling spaces was both commonplace and contentious. Many people openly discussed selling and buying spaces, as Pierre had, but they almost always added caveats. When Ousmane told me he had arrived late and "had to" buy a spot, he also directed that I not let other participants know. When Reggie told me he had sold his spot to a "Spanish" guy up the boardwalk, he added that doing so had made him feel he had sacrificed his integrity. "There's a whole lot of wheeling and dealing," he told me after admitting to the sale. Both men volunteered the information about their purchase without any prodding on my part, but they also found it necessary to justify their behavior.

The practice was therefore largely accepted. Even still, heated complaints over selling spaces often rose to the surface when some other issue was at stake. If longtime participants failed to secure a space during the lottery, tensions flared around the practice, causing people to state that the system was rigged. For instance, Andrea and Barbara did not like each other, and while I never fully clarified the history behind this deep dislike, I saw its effects frequently. When Barbara purchased a space next to Andrea one day, Andrea suddenly threatened to call the police. In conversations about the lottery's effect on the boardwalk, people acted disgusted by the fact that others were selling spaces instead of contributing something meaningful to the marketplace. Yet it never seemed to take long for people to reconcile their reservations and make a sale when they needed it. In essence, selling spaces was accepted, but so was applying informal sanctions to the practice. It very much mattered who was doing the selling and under what circumstances; as a result, it operated both as a tool to boost one's income *and* as a tool for social control that could be called on when needed.

The market for spaces also revealed an entire landscape of meaning on the boardwalk (a topic I dive into further in chapter 5). In setting prices, communicating preferences, and making economic exchanges, people in the boardwalk economy revealed a lot about the way they applied social meaning to the built environment. In fact, knowing the value of certain spaces could be a valuable leveraging tool. It was one of the many ways that acute familiarity with the boardwalk's intricate social and economic landscape served as an enduring form of capital, since there were always new ways to apply such knowledge.

As I sat with a group of musicians at the lottery draw one Tuesday morning, I saw such knowledge put to work. A few musicians had already received a desirable space, and after some discussions about band organization, they were largely comfortable with the arrangement for the upcoming week. But since more ID cards remained in play, there was a possibility to "win" again. And once Reggie's name was called, the conversation turned to how best to do so. As he stood up and began walking to the table, Peter yelled some advice: "The Mexicans like those spots there, one to ten. Get one of those spots, you can sell it." Peter was referring to a group of men who preferred to cluster in a group of spaces at the southern edge of the public marketplace. Earlier in this chapter, we met Raúl and his "cousins," a group of men who often pooled merchandise and used Paco's small inland kiosk to store their goods. Their storage opportunity and close network thus encouraged a stable clustering, which other participants knew and could exploit by choosing one of those spots themselves. Andrea, however, chimed in with a different idea. She said Reggie could instead choose one of the spots north of Westminster, adding that she "worked with people" who would be able to sell those as well. As was common in the later stages of a lottery draw, Reggie would draw on this advice and his own knowledge to choose a space simply for its exchange value, rather than as a space from which to work.

At the lottery another morning, a few people started talking about prices on the boardwalk. Tracy mentioned to Paul that she was trying to get a spot from Chris but he wanted forty dollars for it. She said the going rate is only twenty dollars currently, so somebody would have to talk to Chris about winter rates. Tom walked up a little later and brought up the subject again. Andrea again took a dig at Chris: "Apparently, it depends on who you ask." Tom laughed and added his own take on the matter. "A spot is worth about fifty cents right now," he said.

Knowing exactly what a designated space was worth at a given moment could shift the nature of participation in the permit program, but a person had to be aware of the moving variables when making their assessments. The knowledge that came with long-term participation operated as a clear asset, one that could be harnessed in an exchange with a newcomer who might lack such knowledge.

"Some people are out here just to work the lottery—they don't sell anything on the boardwalk, they sell spaces," Wes told me. But Wes also recounted that a friend of his was approached to sell her space for a hundred dollars. He laughed. "She [the friend] gave it to him for the whole weekend because she felt so bad. And the space was all the way up by Santa Monica!"

Not every space on the boardwalk was as valuable as the next. One had to consider food kiosks and parking lots, distracting music, and bathroom access. Paying one hundred dollars for a space was not only more than a space was worth but was quite ludicrous when that space was located "up by Santa Monica," an area vendors called no-man's-land. Receiving one hundred dollars for a space in this quiet transition zone between the chaotic buzz of Venice and the calmness of Santa Monica was such a skewed transaction, it had caused that vendor some remorse.

One day, I stopped to say hello to Khaled. He told me he was working with a couple of "homeless guys" to help them get set up on the boardwalk. They found some stuff in the garbage, he said to me, adding that the items were "decent" without clarifying exactly what that entailed. As a result, however, Khaled decided to show the guys the ropes, and told them how to display the items to look appealing to customers. But then Khaled laughed and told me he found out one of the men had a lottery ticket. That changed everything, he said. Why hadn't they just sold spot for the day, he had asked them, confounded. "That's an easy fifty bucks!" Khaled laughed again at the absurdity.

There were no hard-and-fast rules, but the market for concrete forced people to think about the value of space in new ways. Represented by a blue ticket in hand, the "designated space" transformed into a tangible commodity. And suddenly, there was a new way to put it to work. Essentially, "a day of work" at the lottery could pay off for people in ways that "a day of work" vending could not—particularly for people who had nothing to vend. In the example above, Khaled's reaction to the men indicated a hierarchy of knowledge like that of Wes's. Khaled found it comical that these men had even thought to spend the day selling discarded objects when they were sitting on easy money by having a ticket for the space in the first place.

Fomenting Resentment and Resistance

The permit program had, in many ways, encouraged people to develop more formal employment relationships with hierarchies shaped by the uneven distribution of both economic and social capital. People began "hiring" one another, doling out commissions, in many cases turning to a large unhoused population that became intricately bound up with the functioning of the marketplace. Even friendships gained new purpose, since they could be leveraged for an extra chance at accessing space and securing income. People began expanding "operations" by selling an "owner's" merchandise from multiple spaces.

The lottery supported the growth of co-ethnic immigrant networks—it allowed people with no prior attachment to the boardwalk a chance to build a business or earn some cash before finding opportunities elsewhere. And because co-ethnic networks shared merchandise that could be conceived as "inextricably intertwined" with one's identity, types of goods became patterned along racial and ethnic lines. As these networks distributed the startup merchandise necessary to make sales, African immigrants became visibly linked to Rasta wear, Latinos to colorful jewelry and intricately painted trinkets, Asians to religious and spiritual figurines.

These shifting positions also sparked animosity, since some believed that playing a numbers game was the wrong way to participate in the marketplace. "Anybody can come—even people who have never been vendors in Venice—and they can get into the lottery!" Randy yelled. He didn't think this was fair; it meant longtime vendors might not get a spot. "The real problem here is immigration, [the city doesn't] ask for any IDs or papers, so these guys can come in and work for free, and not pay any taxes." Then he noted the big issue: "Plus, they have so large of a network that they are almost always guaranteed a spot." He told me how "they" come over with their entire family and everybody in their family would get a ticket, so of course they would get a spot. He continued, "The INS really needs to come up in here."

Kenny also resented the commercialism that the lottery appeared to foster. It was a "swap meet," he told me, using a common reference to indicate a perceived negative shift from artwork to commercial goods. For Kenny, the lottery had sparked a new environment that, as he said, wasn't "really Venice." Instead, it was a space of "desperation."

For Mila, who worked retail on the east side of the boardwalk, the conflicts that resulted from the system were troublesome. But she did not necessarily place blame on the distribution system. "Those guys fight a lot," she said of the musicians, arguing that they created a negative atmosphere and contrasting them with others whom she felt were "good people."

The city's version of "equitable" access did not eliminate hierarchies and inequities; these merely took new shape, producing a different set of "winners" and "losers." Vendors who had been working on the boardwalk for years saw the value of seniority diminish (though not disappear) and physical intimidation could not translate easily into ownership over space. Instead, there was strength in numbers, and a full network of people in need could itself be an asset. A market for designated spaces emerged, constructing new ways to earn income and offering a new outlet to turn one's familiarity with the social world of the marketplace into profit. Immigrants with no history of working on the boardwalk could find the opportunity for a temporary springboard. An unhoused population could gain new inroads into the economy. New opportunities for income met with new forms of exploitation, as navigating one set of precarious conditions could simply create another.

In the end, as people strove to meet their needs in the context of the permit program, they shaped the boardwalk marketplace in ways that created visible links between the urban landscape and broader social issues left unresolved by failed and inadequate social systems.[9] As a result, when town halls and neighborhood council meetings erupted in conflict over what to do with the boardwalk, the conversation typically centered on the symptoms of much bigger social issues, like homelessness, ineffective immigration policy, mental health issues, and unfettered commercialism. Even while Venice was publicly celebrated as a place with bohemian roots and a strong appreciation for its racial and socioeconomic diversity, the nature of regulation—and people's attempt to meet their needs in the face of it—allowed new boundaries and resentments to coalesce.[10]

But, as this book continues to show, the subversive safety net was always in the making, and workers exhibited a form of agency. In fact, many working here did not passively accept the conditions that structured their opportunity for income generation. They actively shaped them. In the final years of the permit program, a group of participants filed a lawsuit against the city. With the expertise of one participant who had worked in the legal field prior to the boardwalk and bolstered by the legendary status of past successful lawsuits, they argued that the Public Expression Participant Permit Program was unconstitutional. And while they largely argued that this unconstitutionality rested in the program's denial of their free speech rights, the case itself centered on the program's vagueness and enforceability.[11] On October 21, 2010, the court granted in part their motion for a preliminary injunction. And with that ruling, the boardwalk returned to the first-come-first-served rule of access.

Once again, people were encouraged to adopt new (and old) strategies to ensure their access to space. The precarious life circumstances and characteristics that may have been harnessed as resources during the permit program were not equally transferable to the new system. Similarly, a different set of characteristics and precarious circumstances would suddenly gain value. Partnerships and co-ethnic networks continued to provide opportunities for access, but in different ways. New ways to conceive of ownership developed, sparking new forms of control for some and new forms of exclusion for others.

From Playing the Lottery to Building the Block

On the morning after the injunction, I watched as Hazel walked briskly to an LAPD sedan parked just off the boardwalk. I overheard her ask the officer to "keep an eye out"; she anticipated a fight, she said. I heard her explain to the officer that she had moved her artwork to the space on the northern corner of the block—a space she knew another vendor preferred.

After Hazel left, I walked up to the officer and asked her about the change. She told me in no uncertain terms she was there that morning to manage what was likely to be "bedlam," adding, "You know how it is with first-come-first-served."

Aside from the months before Memorial Day, when the designated P zone operated under first-come-first-served, I really didn't know how it was. There were rumors of fights, though I had never witnessed a physical altercation over access to spaces. And seeing the first-come-first-served approach play out during winter months—for only one segment of the pathway and in an overall context of the permit program—was not the same as watching the entire permit program vanish. In fact, many of the people I had come to know, like Matías, Emilio, Juan, and Ousmane, had all made major inroads during the permit program. How would they adjust? And if first-come-first-served was so intimidating, how would mild-mannered participants like Ricardo fare? Or women like Hazel?

Some of those effects were felt quickly, as when Diego told me that the need for people to reserve spaces in the early-morning hours was quite different from the need for people to throw an extra ID card into the lottery draw on Tuesday mornings. Kinship networks were not immediately transferable. "I'd have my wife come to the lottery. But I'm not having my wife come out here at two a.m.," he said, referring to the relatively extreme tactic some employed to reserve a space for a weekend during the summer peak season. For those with cash but little family, the lottery had encouraged people to partner up and pay for extra ID cards. As we saw with Tim and RJ, this created opportunity as well as exploitation for folks who were unhoused. Without the need for RJ's ID card, the partnership was no longer so valuable for Tim. In other words, social capital continued to be important, but it changed form. And in Diego's case, he indicated that his wife may have served as a resource for securing a space in the lottery, but she was no longer a resource for securing a space during first-come-first-served.

Furthermore, the permit program and lottery had bolstered the idea that the spaces themselves—which had been delineated by painted borders and marked with a number—could be exchanged for money. The tangibility of the "ticket" supported the idea that there was, in fact, a commodity at stake. For the five years of the permit program and lottery, the sense of ownership over space had been both tangible and unstable, since one's ability to hold a blue ticket rested on a weekly chance of "winning." But such claims making changed with the end of permit program, and therefore altered the way people could extract income from a designated space.

After the lottery ended, a different sense of ownership over space reemerged, one that was no longer based on a blue ticket. I witnessed the return of the block, as people tried to stabilize their access by claiming clusters of spaces with a group of regular participants. The same day that Hazel was nervous about a possible conflict over space, others were cheering. And the reason for their exuberance was a consistent sense of freedom to establish new forms of ownership over specific clusters of spaces. The upheaval caused by the weekly lottery could be countered.

When Randy walked up to his favorite spot next to Tim, he was bursting with energy. He yelled to Tim, "Did you hear about the ruling?! Now we can do anything!" The two slapped hands. Tim looked around the block where he and Randy usually set up and said, "We own this!" Even Farid, the jewelry merchant on the inland side of the boardwalk, celebrated this new form of control, because he could now place an empty table in the space across from his store, he told me. It would simply act to sit there and keep any competition at bay—Matías would not so easily compete with his sales. Anthony smiled widely. "Lotterization was illegal," he yelled. There was clear pride in having fought the system and won, further fueling people's attachment to the boardwalk as a meaningful site of resistance and interpreting their participation in the marketplace as active, agential, and impactful.

But such transitions were not seamless. People had become quite attached to the forms of power they had held and the way their own resources translated into success. In the return to first-come-first-served, some people would find that the meaning they had attached to relationships would shift. Greater security for some became greater insecurity for others. And though shifts could be socially and materially significant for individual participants, these moments of transition also showed how the subversive safety net—always in dialogue with state regulation—remained dynamic.

On my way to the coffee shop, I saw Tim sitting in the driver's seat of his parked car. "Hi," I said.

"Hey," he replied, exhaling a plume of smoke from his joint out the window. He seemed sleepy but told me he was getting ready to set up.

"How was your night?" I asked.

"Fine," he said. He had gone home right after work the day before, but then woke up at 2:30 that morning and decided to come down and get a couple of spots. He laughed a little and said, "I bumped RJ [to the next block]."

I thought of RJ, who was livid the day before after Tim failed to save him a spot. The two had been working together through the lottery, and I knew RJ had some expectations about their partnership. But since Tim referenced "a couple" of spots, I inquired for more information.

"Are you going to give one of those spots to RJ?" I asked.

"No," he said, "I'm going to do a double-wide." In other words, he would be setting up business on two adjacent spaces.

Maybe he sensed some judgment from me. Or maybe he just knew it was a selfish choice. Either way, Tim continued. "RJ went down to the other block and marked thirty-four," he said, referring to the commonly accepted placement of a chair, box, or other solid object on the concrete. "But somebody offered him money for it, so he sold it and went back to sleep. He's asleep in the van now."

Tim seemed confident that this was the end of things. However, in the time it took me to buy a coffee and walk back outside, it was clear that things were far from resolved.

Randy and RJ walked by me toward the boardwalk, arguing aggressively about something I couldn't quite understand. They walked up to spot 34—the spot that RJ had allegedly sold before returning to sleep. Only now, spot 34 was surrounded by two parked LAPD sedans. A few other officers stood nearby, and a crowd had gathered. It was Khaled, however, who was the center of attention. "You can't sell a spot!" Khaled boomed at RJ.

When Randy chimed in, it was with the awareness that RJ should be a member of his own block just north of the one that contained spot 34. "I would've given RJ the money if that's what he needed!" Randy yelled as he walked back to his own spot.

Khaled did not end things there, though. He stood with his legs wide apart, his torso leaning toward RJ, and yelled forcefully: "You can't come here and sell this spot! You guys are down there, not here!" He lifted his arm and motioned north. "You are over on that block!" Khaled boomed again.

RJ walked out of the group quickly, his head down. As he passed me, he muttered, "It was a moment of weakness."

Khaled yelled after him, "If that were the case, I'd be rich by now!"

The scene above is as complex as it is revealing. It is a moment of interaction through which the vendors make visible a shift in the process by which people accessed space appropriately, claimed ownership over space, and used that space. RJ was operating on a prior system of access and ownership, one that Khaled himself had clearly accepted earlier when he stood dumbfounded by the fact that a couple of men had not sold their space in lieu of working. So, RJ had chosen a space based on its seeming availability—in other words, it was not physically marked or occupied—and he believed this imparted to him the same ownership and control over the space that a blue ticket would have afforded him, which included the right to sell it. What he did not consider (or if he did, he did not heed it) was the fact that the rules of ownership had fundamentally changed, calling into question any claim to money exchanged for the space.

Through this interaction, Khaled communicated that "groups" of people, rather than individuals, could lay claim to certain blocks. Even though RJ was alone in his breach, Khaled yelled "*You guys* are down there, not here!" He also indicated that any claim to profit for a space was reserved for people who "belonged" on that block.

Perhaps the greatest confirmation of this shift was the broad agreement of RJ's breach. The scene above did not unfold as a person-to-person conflict in which Khaled argued for one form of access to space while RJ offered another. Quite the contrary; what we witnessed was a growing consensus of the meaning of the situation. Upon confrontation, RJ admitted the gaff, stating, "It was a moment of weakness." Furthermore, Randy recognized that RJ should have never left *their* block and moved south, even indicating a willingness to support RJ financially ("I would've given RJ the ten dollars if that's what he needed!") so that he would not have had to commit such an infraction.

As a final indication of agreement, the LAPD officers did nothing to calm Khaled's anger, and while he was physically and vocally the center of the scene, he was not coerced into ending the argument. They merely waited for RJ to leave the scene, purposefully or inadvertently providing an official stamp of approval on the resolution. Such an interaction therefore indicated that change was possible, and that for all the remorse RJ experienced in that moment, there was a collective commitment to settle on new ways of claiming access to space.

Over time, claims like those of Khaled, Randy, and Tim proved solid. The user-to-space consistency was almost mind-boggling in comparison to the constant reorganization of spaces seen during the permit program. Such consistency even allowed for new group endeavors to arise, such that neighboring users could "go in" on merchandise together or set up larger side-by-side operations, as Tim had suggested early with his use of the term *double-wide*. They could also use spaces in more innovative ways, as when Rennie and Chuck set up a little "art store" of commercial products in the small area spanning two spaces. In addition, blocks provided the opportunity for clusters of participants to protect one another's access to space and create more localized guidelines for appropriate behavior.

Andrea sat down at her table, her tarot cards spread across a soft red fabric, and told me in her frank demeanor, "We've pretty much got our block worked out." It had been months since the permit program and lottery system ended, and she proceeded to tell me what *worked out* meant to her. For one, she noted that the group of people setting up on the block was consistent, or in other words, the spaces had been returned to "regulars." It was because of this consistency, she said, that the group now had control over the types of activities taking place there. When a vendor tried to set up with bracelets earlier in the day, Andrea recounted that everybody "got them to leave"—the reason being a disconnect between the newcomer's goods and the preferred style of vending on the block. "We can keep the commercial shit out," she said.

Each block had a slightly different way of organizing, and while such processes were not without moments of contestation, they helped stabilize the boardwalk as a coherent whole. In fact, people typically communicated satisfaction with their own blocks in comparison to perceived issues on "other" blocks. For instance, Timmy told me that things were "mostly worked out here," referring to his block. "Down there," he motioned south, there were problems, and "up there," he motioned north, "they've mostly worked things out, but they're setting it up to have too many people," he noted. "Here, it's quiet."

Some blocks were known for "drama," some for commercial goods (or "crap," depending on who you asked), and others for original artwork and music. The smaller clusters of likeminded participants allowed different strategies for access to coalesce. Emilio, one of the many immigrants who had arrived and seen some success during the permit program, had to change his tactics somewhat when the program disappeared. His block used a rotating system for saving spots. "It's my turn to sleep here," he told me. His own way of keeping down the competition for space was to limit awareness of the opportunities on the boardwalk. "In LA, they tell them that they can make money here, that the first to arrive gets the spot," he told me. "Who tells them?" I asked. "In downtown," he responded vaguely, "when they go downtown, people tell them." He recounted that a Puerto Rican woman came to him to ask what time she'd need to be there to set up. He told her about 6 or 7 a.m. Then he smirked at me and said, "I come at five."

Emilio's narrative illustrates that social networks remained important, but the way people could put them to work changed. A group of people could take turns saving spots on a given block rather than throwing additional ID cards into the lottery. In addition, exchanging money for spaces was no longer linked to the lottery's blue ticket.

Conclusion

Though settings and regulatory contexts for street-level economic activities differ in their particularities, the ongoing negotiation between opportunity and constraint remains. People find ways to use public space for their own economic survival, often in the face of local regulation and policies.[12] People are also creative; sometimes they find new opportunities for street-level economic activity in the application of regulation that may have been enacted to limit those very activities.[13]

On the boardwalk, people fought to produce a workplace from this public space, weaving an initial strand of the subversive safety net. But the social world here was dynamic, and while shifting social relations led to different hierarchies, they rarely solidified. The rules of the game simply changed too often. New configurations of advantage and disadvantage formed and dissolved. People may have been resilient in their efforts to meet their needs, but so too were the precarious conditions that shaped those needs. Safety nets are rarely equitable, and this subversive safety net was no different. It continued to be woven through practices of making precarity work that mitigated, exploited, and exacerbated the precarious conditions people faced.

The injunction brought an end to the weekly reorganization imposed by the lottery, alongside all the opportunity and upheaval it brought with it. Now "the block" became the most important sociospatial construct on the boardwalk. And rather than a completely new development, the primacy of the block was often discussed as a return to the way things were before the lottery and permit program began—a return to "regulars." It was, in fact, both more stable and more exclusionary. Up and down the boardwalk, people echoed the role of "the block" in allowing for the formation of smaller communities of workers. Khaled announced, "This is the crew!" Karissa told me that further north, "we're like a family up here."

Positive portrayals of "the block," "the crew," and "a family" hint at important constructions of community on the boardwalk. But how did such community coalesce? And what role did it play? In the next chapter, I examine an additional practice of making precarity work: the practice by which people cultivate a community of workers. This practice of making precarity work weaves another vital strand of the subversive safety net, allowing people to mitigate the daily uncertainty that comes with informal precarious work and access some semblance of protections they are otherwise unable to access through employment.

3

Cultivating a Community of Workers

It was 7 o'clock on Friday morning and the beach was cloaked with a morning fog. Emma stood against the outside wall of the pizza shop, staring into the distance while she smoked a cigarette and sipped a cup of coffee. Her car sat next to her, piled over five feet high with tables, art supplies, paintings, and small sculptures. It was the body of work she had cultivated over the years, and the body of work from which she supported herself and her son. On the block just north, a couple of men stirred in their sleeping bags, slowly gathering their belongings before LAPD officers began issuing tickets. The wooden screen door of Groundwork creaked and banged intermittently as people made their way in and out of the coffee shop; some were dressed for the office, others in pajamas, a few wrapped in wool blankets. Joggers and power walkers cut through the gray with their brightly colored spandex and winded conversations.

Emma finished her cigarette, threw the butt in the trash, and grabbed her skateboard. Then she pushed away, leaving her cart and all its contents behind.

Emma had worked on the boardwalk for the better part of a decade. Even still, she often told me the boardwalk was "not her life," distancing herself from the place where she averaged twelve-hour days, five to seven days a week. "It's just me and my son. I don't know anybody, and nobody knows me." But Emma's actions seemed to tell a different story. In a place described as "proudly unpredictable," she appeared confident and comfortable leaving vital belongings unattended on the open concrete. It was the kind of puzzling contradiction that seemed to indicate something else might be happening, and that Emma might "see" the situation in ways invisible to the untrained eye. What, then, might have informed her actions?

In the previous chapter, we saw people organize socially to navigate constraints over access that stemmed from the city's conception of public-space usage and "equitable access." But those working here asserted their own conception, one that allowed the formation of ownership over space and the ability to earn income from it. And while we saw the development of small groups, networks, and blocks, each appeared in isolation from one another. In this chapter, I show how the practice of making precarity work entails cultivating a broader community of workers, and I show how these workers form another vital strand of the subversive safety net. To do this, I burrow specifically into the interactions through which this community was formed, how relationships gained meaning, and how these relationships became highly consequential for building and maintaining stability in a place with zero guarantees. Here we find a key social mechanism: trust.

Sociologists have long contended with this slippery yet significant concept. Trust is bound up in the very way we understand our environments.[1] For any concerted action to take place, people must pull from a common set of sense-making tools and consequently, interpret a given situation in similar ways. Trust is part of how people come to read objects, identities, and actions as familiar. It is part of how people perceive their surroundings as normal.[2] It is also a collective practice, as people interpret routinized interactions as a type of order that engenders feelings of safety.[3]

In many ways, the boardwalk was fertile ground for trust. After all, the marketplace along the pathway's western edge was a type of ephemeral event; it was constructed anew each morning and deconstructed each evening. There was no management. No stalls to rent. No guarantees of place or pay. Trust often becomes most robust in the face of uncertainty.

And yet, trust here had many strikes against it. There was an ever-changing cast of characters mulling about—an ongoing presence of young runaways, backpackers, visitors, and tourists. One could never be too sure of such perpetual strangers, their intentions, their ability to make common sense of the scene. In addition, even longtime participants disappeared and reappeared. Cell phone numbers changed, if they existed at all. Addresses could be momentary. Names were unofficial. People moved in and out of jail. People suffered dependency to drugs and alcohol. People exhibited a range of mental health problems. Many even expressed a stance of general distrust, as happens when people carry with them negative experiences of the very institutions aimed to alleviate such issues.[4]

Furthermore, those common bonds viewed as conducive to trust were largely missing. People here were diverse in racial and ethnic identity, legal status, place of residence, education, and other life conditions. As we have seen, the Free Speech Zone offered such a rare opportunity for economic participation that it drew a vastly diverse crowd. Remember again that people here were hippies and homeless, defected corporate employees and undocumented immigrants. They were ex-gang members and single mothers, art students and alcoholics. They straddled barriers in language, class, race, ethnicity, religion, education, and more. And yet, somehow, they came together each day to construct this marketplace. How, then, might trust operate here? How did it forge a community of workers? And how did this community form a part of the subversive safety net?

Sitting between a Rock and a Hard Place

Despite all the invocations of autonomy and individualism I heard, working on the boardwalk was not a solitary affair. Even the most reclusive participants relied on others to know well enough to let them be. Every facet of work was shaped by its generally precarious and informal nature, as well as the life conditions that people brought with them; every facet involved interaction and exchange with others. And the very needs that required interaction and exchange reared their heads quickly, allowing little time for people to fully assess one another's intentions.

I met a man one morning when he walked around the corner rolling a small cart full of stones and jewelry. It was a weekday, in a lull between spring break and summer, and the block was relatively empty. The man parked his cart on the east side, where I was already sitting on a stool, waiting to set up. A woman I did not recognize walked by, her long flowing skirt trailing behind her. The man began yelling at her, and she returned the ire.

I must assume that the man believed the public nature of this argument warranted some explanation, because his first words to me were "She's my ex." Unprompted, he then launched into the story of their road to the boardwalk. He told me how the two had met in Miami and worked as vendors for a couple of years. They had spent the past year driving their van across the country, and now in Venice, they had just broken up. "She's got my stuff hostage," he said.

It was a sparse showing that morning—not wholly surprising, since it was a weekday and not a particularly tourist-heavy part of the year. I was rather unsurprised, then, when the man made it to 9 o'clock without any interference from regulars. Manuel, Paul, Umar, and Ricardo were all no-shows, and I was not going to interfere. So, the man and I moved our belongings to the west side and set up a couple of spaces from each other. As I unpacked, he walked over to me.

"Kevin," he said as he held out his hand.

"Laura," I responded.

Kevin reached into his small cart and pulled out some rough stones. He had recently cut them, he told me, to make pendants for necklaces. While we spoke, his ex-girlfriend walked back and forth on the pathway yelling at him to return her stuff or she would be throwing his backpack in the dumpster. Apparently, Kevin wasn't the only one whose stuff was being held hostage.

"She's all drama," he told me.

After we unpacked, Kevin came back over to my space and asked if I'd watch his things while he went to shave. I agreed, and he walked toward the public bathrooms about five hundred feet out on the beach. In doing so, he left all his belongings with me, a woman he had just met, all while his ex-girlfriend was roaming around threatening to destroy everything he owned. But when Kevin returned, he flashed me a big smile, his face freshly shaven and his merchandise untouched.

Kevin's request was a relatively defined exchange: he asked me directly to look after his belongings and let me know where he'd be and what he'd be doing. Kevin likely drew from a set of cues that informed his decision. I looked the part of a vendor, sitting on the east side of the boardwalk with my cart, waiting for the 9 a.m. setup time. Kevin may have assumed that we shared a similar set of vulnerabilities. As a woman, I may have seemed unthreatening. I did not provide any indication of untrustworthiness (or trustworthiness, for that matter), during our conversation. I smiled and nodded when he spoke to me about his life—a friendly response that may have informed his decision about how to act. Still, he made himself vulnerable by leaving his belongings out on the open concrete, asking a woman he'd just met to "keep an eye."

Vendors like Kevin often arrived with bins full of merchandise. It took people as much as an hour to set up their displays—and more if the display was an intricate sand sculpture. It was not practical, then, for a person to take these items with them should they have to leave the space—and needing to leave was a guarantee. People needed to use the restroom. They needed to purchase lunch. They needed to run errands. But as they did, their belongings remained without them. For those who had newly arrived, there was little time to fully assess others in making these quick decisions. For newcomers like Kevin, trust was a particular leap of faith. They had not had time to learn all the cues to inform an accurate reading of the boardwalk. Kevin's vulnerability therefore stemmed, in part, from him being a new arrival.

However, given the constant flow of new people, even vendors who had spent years on the boardwalk found themselves in moments where they were required to make quick decisions with limited information.

One day, I came out to the boardwalk to find Jorge sitting on a stool with all of Randy's artwork around him. It was a bit odd, since last I knew of it, Anthony, a white man with a beaming smile and serious drinking habit, had been working to sell for Randy while he did the festival circuit. Jorge had grown up in Venice and was one of the most kindhearted people I met during my research. After a job loss and a growing dependence on alcohol, he was now unhoused. I first met him when he began hanging around Tim and his crew for some time, but he had been neither a vendor nor an odd-job worker. So, I was surprised to see him in the new role.

"Are you selling for Randy now?" I asked.

"Anthony got drunk and started yelling the n-word," Jorge told me. "He was fired."

I had heard comments from Anthony in the past, mostly under-the-breath statements lamenting the fact that he was a white man working for a Black man—an ongoing reminder that even when people are in need, they can be remiss to let go of the unearned privilege to which they cling. And Randy was not just any artist—he was a Black artist whose paintings highlighted the work of Black intellectuals. He had limits, and it was unsurprising that he had reached them.

"Randy was really between a rock and a hard place," Jorge told me. "He had twelve hours to make a decision." According to Jorge, it only took one question: "He asked me if he could trust me, and I said yes—you could ask anybody on the boardwalk," drawing on the community as a resource.

Still, Jorge admitted, the job was somewhat of a surprise. "Normally I've only hung out here. Randy didn't really know me," he said.

"Well, how's it going?" I asked.

"Good, I've been averaging about a hundred dollars a day with Randy's stuff," he said proudly.

In all fairness, that was not all profit for Jorge; the commission was 30 percent. But over the following months, Randy's decision proved to be mutually beneficial. Jorge "cleaned up" Randy's display. He laid out pieces of turf on the concrete and created an open-U-shaped space that the customer could step into. The display transformed the once-passive observation of artwork into a more engaged gallery setting. When police officers walked by and complimented Jorge on the new look, he turned to me with his characteristic grin. He was proud to be earning money and receiving some "fringe benefits"—specifically a car to sleep in at night and some meals here and there.

Randy acknowledged that he was pleased too. "After Anthony, I needed God to send a clean employee," he told me. "And I got Jorge."

Jorge discussed the way Randy's decision emerged from a pressing need to keep his profit going and maintain his access to the boardwalk. Again, being bound to the boardwalk sparked an important and immediate form of trust. And through a quick interaction, Randy and Jorge went from people without any real knowledge of each other into a relationship that placed each of them in vulnerable positions by establishing an informal set of expectations. Though Jorge was paid a small commission for his effort, there was no contract, no credentialing, and no way for Randy to establish official knowledge of Jorge's identity or home address. In addition, Jorge's alcohol dependency was in the open, and he frequently started drinking by late afternoon.

Over the years, I witnessed many similar relationships develop quickly. And as can often be the case under such precarious circumstances, these quickly formed social ties provided a bevy of resources.[5] People shared access to showers, food, rides, merchandise, and places to sleep. In the case of Jorge and Randy, Jorge gained an income and Randy had the freedom to pursue other venues for his artwork. Many nights, Jorge could sleep in Randy's van, temporarily getting him off the street (a form of support that I examine further in the next chapter).

But Randy did not profess to trust Jorge in some general sense. Rather, Randy's actions indicated a belief that Jorge would make similar sense of this new business arrangement and act accordingly. Still, trust was an important part of taking these actions, and it did important work to navigate these immediate needs.

Part of making precarity work is about making quick decisions to turn to others and ask for help. Regardless of the speed with which such requests took place in the boardwalk marketplace, trust did important foundational work. It transformed the people present and available into an active and consequential community of workers. Furthermore, Jorge pulled from referrals within the community to inform Randy's decision when he stated, "You could ask anybody on the boardwalk." The community itself became a resource: in Jorge's case, for the acquisition of an odd job, and in Randy's case, for a worker who could assist him as he met other needs.

Kevin and Randy both turned to relative strangers for vital assistance. But the conditions of work on the boardwalk allowed these interactions to develop over time, particularly as they were forced into ongoing contact. These were the face-to-face moments during which people had to turn to one another when they found themselves between a rock and a hard place. And such pressing needs continued to arise. As a result, people continued to make themselves vulnerable to one another to manage immediate needs; they also continued to meet the needs of others. Following people over time, we see how such interactions become routinized, building a more stable social order.[6]

When a tourist arrived with a fifty-dollar bill, Umar turned to see if Paul had change. When Paul had to use the bathroom, he had to ask Leia to pay attention to customers and make any sales that came his way. These behaviors happened rather quickly, as people worked side by side over the course of time. Again, such behaviors did important work to sustain people's access to space and income.

They also set the stage for the formation of deeper expectations and more significant outcomes. When Ricardo realized he did not have enough cash to make change for a sale, he turned to see if I had a ten-dollar bill. I held up my open palms to motion that I was out. Umar worked in the spot next to me and saw the interaction. He stood up, walked over to Ricardo, and handed a ten-dollar bill across the table. After providing the customer with change, Ricardo left from behind his table and jogged across the pathway to Noah's nearby store. He quickly returned, walked over to Umar's table, and handed him back a ten-dollar bill.

If Ricardo, like most of the workers here, wanted to earn enough income to make ends meet, he would have to figure out how to capitalize on each sale. Accurate change was difficult to ensure when working in this type of a tourist destination. International tourists often carried fifty-dollar or one-hundred-dollar bills, and many vendors sold their goods for two to ten dollars. Given that most workers had to spend most of their earnings, they were often left in an ongoing struggle to keep a stock of cash on hand. For Ricardo, the way to manage the issue was to engage the assistance of both Umar and Noah. Umar offered Ricardo a signal that he did, in fact, have cash on hand and was willing to step in and offer it to help Ricardo. Noah, the nearby merchant, also helped by offering Ricardo change from the cash register. As people requested and made change, they became vulnerable to one another, and furthermore vulnerable to a larger community privy to public displays of cash on hand.

Throughout the day, nearly every person working on the boardwalk found themselves with a need to leave their space. And even on days when people knew they would be away for long stretches of time, they were still motivated to set up. Khaled put out empty tables one day to ensure people knew the space "belonged" to him. Leia and Manuel set up their tables one morning and left for a leisurely breakfast. Paul set up his tables knowing he'd spend the better part of the day biking to Santa Monica to purchase a couple of blank canvases. They were aware that if they wanted ongoing access to the boardwalk, they should not allow their space to appear available for too long. We can understand why participants may have more easily left their belongings unattended than their space unclaimed, having learned of the difficulty of access in the previous chapter. Still, leaving one's merchandise sitting idle was not just a risk of theft, it was also a risk of lost income.

Paul had been working along the Venice boardwalk on and off for over five years. After only a few days of my working next to him, he stood up and walked over to my table. "Come with me," he said, walking the couple of feet over to his own table. I stood next to him as he began pointing, quickly rattling off prices. "These are four dollars, these ten, these twenty-five, these over here are seven, these ten. I'll be right back."

Paul needed to use the restroom. But if he was to be successful on the boardwalk, he knew he should also capitalize on every potential sale. This tension sparked new interactions and exchanges so that Paul could ensure continued profit in his absence. The exchange was not without risk. In fact, though I occasionally sold merchandise here and there for Paul, he remained vulnerable not only to opportunism but to mistakes. Paul's table was full of a diverse set of items, from jewelry to statues to artwork, many of which varied in size and material. At one point, for instance, I handed him five dollars for a small figurine I had sold in his absence—the price he quoted me for similar items. What I failed to realize was the difference in weight and material of the figurine I sold, which he had valued at twenty dollars. "Oh no," he said. Still, he shrugged it off, smiling rather than getting angry. Later, I told Paul I'd be right back, vacating my spot for about ten minutes. Upon my return, he handed me twenty-five dollars, the full amount for which I sold my items. These exchanges required a collective effort, as people counted on one another to step up and fulfill the expectations others had of them.

When Paul left for the bathroom again, I kept an eye on his table. A woman picked up a bracelet, and I realized I did not remember the price. Worried about my past mistake, I took it over to Umar, who was finishing with a customer. I held up the bracelet.

"Ten dollars," Umar said.

I ran back to the table and told the customer. She handed me a twenty-dollar bill. Knowing I did not have the cash on hand, I looked back at Umar.

"You need change?" he asked. I asked for two tens and handed Umar the twenty.

Paul walked back from the bathroom, and I handed him the ten.

"Thanks," he said.

Soon afterward, I walked a couple of blocks to my nearby apartment and returned about twenty minutes later.

"Give me five dollars," Paul said when I returned, handing me thirty.

"I don't have it on me," I said, and assured him I would get it to him soon.

"Fine, give it to me later."

As soon as I made another sale, I handed the five dollars back to Paul.

Moments like these illustrate the intricate ballet of assistance and requests needed to keep the boardwalk economy rolling. At times, it was quite inspiring to watch. But inviting people to deal with your cash was not free from problems. People made mistakes; inventory could be lost. In each of these cases, people were managing immediate needs that arose during work. They turned to others for help, regardless of how well they knew them, and made themselves vulnerable. For example, when Jorge took over sales for Randy, he also gave Randy control over his own ability to make cash. Trusting in others helped people manage short-term needs. These were also important moments in which people could illustrate that they too understood such interactions in similar ways.

Cultivating Expectations and Long-Term Support

It was still quiet around 11 o'clock—the crowds had yet to arrive, and the few people walking were not buying. Khaled walked off to Zelda's on the corner to buy a few clam chowders. He gave one to me, which I naively declined, and one to Paul.

"We all eat together," Khaled said. It was "his turn" to buy lunch, he told me, specifically because Paul had bought it the past few weeks. "It's really my turn."

Khaled looked over to the man next to me making jewelry and offered him the extra soup. I did not know this vendor well, but following the donation, Khaled seemed quite confident that the soup would initiate some reciprocity. "I bet you later he gives me something," he told me, "You just watch."

Later in the day, I returned from a quick walk and looked at Khaled. He had a pile of peanuts in front him and was shelling them and popping them into his mouth. When he saw me, he laughed. "I told you!" he said as he pointed to the peanuts.

The circulation of food among participants may seem like background activity, but if we look more closely at seemingly mundane moments of collective action, we find that people here were cultivating more long-term expectations that reinforced the subversive safety net. For instance, the exchange of food operated as an important tool to establish expectations and begin building commonality. That is, "We all eat together" cultivated a sense of "we-ness" among those working here. In fact, my own declination of clam chowder emerged as so consequential that when I later accepted food from Paul, who directly offered me homemade falafel, it sparked an emotionally charged argument with Khaled about my earlier failure to show him appropriate respect and act as part of the community. In a marketplace constructed largely on the individual—personal expression, first-come-first-served, one-person-one-space—these moments did important work to sustain trust between those working here. My own gaff made that painfully clear.

Again, we can return to the temporal aspects of trust. People had to decide on the duration of a given interaction or exchange, consequently shaping the type of relationship that resulted. Here we might think of the nature and role of expectations on the boardwalk. The people working here built such expectations, and thereby trust, through the accumulation of small exchanges, moments of vulnerability, and repetitive interactions.[7] These processes cultivated a community of workers that then formed a vital part of the subversive safety net.

At 7:30 in the morning, I walked past a rather quiet coffee shop and turned the corner onto the boardwalk. The block was empty, but along the western edge, each "designated space" was marked with a cardboard box. The space I had been setting up on recently was marked with a gray paint can. In some ways, I had "inherited" the space, after working as a partner to one of the vendors who had been arrested for possible assault. I dropped my stool next to the can, placing it in the sand behind the space, and walked south to get the cart from storage. I ran into Raúl along the way, who told me he and Ricardo had saved the spaces for us last night. Sure enough, the paint can was Raúl's doing. At 8 a.m., Paul came around the corner pushing his cart, piled high with bins and canvases, and placed them in front of Mr. Park's souvenir store.

"Are you here?" Paul asked me, pointing to the paint can.

I told him, "I'll go there," adding that I didn't really care which space I took for the day.

He agreed I should "go there," pointing to the paint can and my stool. "I'll go here," he said, pointing to an adjacent space in which Umar typically worked, and "Ricardo will go there," he said, pointing just south of my own space.

Within about thirty minutes, Ricardo arrived, wheeling his own cart to the eastern edge. "Is this me?" he said, pointing to the space where Paul had now placed some of his own plastic bins.

"Yes," he said, repeating the roster of people lined up for the day.

Soon afterward, Leia, a woman who worked with her husband, Manuel, walked onto the boardwalk and set a chair down against the storefront just north of us. She walked over to Paul and me to say hello. She looked across to the west side and commented that Paul would get to be next to her today, since Umar was not coming until next week. At 9 a.m., we all walked west and began sweeping up the sand on the concrete, setting up tables and chairs, and unpacking merchandise.

By following individuals as they organized the block, we see how those working here not only built positive expectations of one another through ongoing interaction but also came to interpret and anticipate one another's expectations and future cooperation. Here, we can see that trust did the work of constructing more long-term economic stability. When Paul said, "Ricardo will go there" as he surveyed the spaces available, he illustrated his own expectation of Ricardo's future cooperation. Ricardo's behavior also indicated his expectations of the group, since he arrived and verified with Paul, "Is this me?" Ricardo approached others and was happy to oblige them, further allowing block organization to emerge as a communal act. It was clear that upon arrival those expectations were already in place, and what unfolded was an expression of and meeting of those expectations.

The consequences of such interactions became both interpersonally and materially significant. As people organized the block, they built the conditions for interaction to become routinized in a workplace premised on potential turnover. In predicting and interpreting one another's expectations, this collective act turned the first-come-first-served policy into a first-come-many-served policy.

The development of this type of reciprocity and expectation was important because it allowed people a way to rely on their environment to provide stability. In fact, these types of exchanges and expectations made the seemingly chaotic boardwalk rather predictable. Khaled was even playing with this knowledge of predictability when he told me in reference to expectations of food, "You just watch." But Khaled also knew that this kind of benefit came with a price, and that entering these exchanges meant a person also owed something in return. For instance, one day I agreed to help Khaled sell some of his merchandise while he left to run errands. I did not recognize the man working next to me, and quickly asked Khaled if he knew the man. "He's fine," he told me. But then he provided an important caveat: "Don't go making friends, though; I may need his spot one day."

Making precarity work is often about walking this line, since the subversive safety net cannot support all. While reciprocity can be a wonderful thing, it can also limit a person's ability to act in their own interest. It is a balance of needs, and in establishing a community of workers, participants considered the risks and benefits of these relationships. Merely being present was not enough to be a part of the community of workers, and furthermore, fellow workers were not necessarily friends.

"Who is the singer?" I asked Paul one day. "He's new," he told me, explaining that other vendors had "let him on the block" because he was a temporary gig. This way, when Rennie returned from his day off, he'd still have his spot.

Paul, Ricardo, and others had used the temporary presence of this new singer to protect Rennie's long-term presence. Such behaviors allowed the boardwalk to remain dynamic, but they also controlled the kind of turnover possible. Keeping a small group of people with whom one has built up a pattern of collective behavior and a growing set of expectations was vital. It was this community that helped provide the kind of long-term security rarely offered in such forms of precarious work.

One day I noticed that Umar had not been at work for a few days. Leia had mentioned he would not be working that weekend, but come Tuesday, he had still not returned. As I watched Leia unpacking her own merchandise, I saw her begin to set up Umar's artwork as well, using about three-quarters of the table for his goods and one-quarter to display her own. I asked her what was going on. She told me Umar was quite sick, but at least this way he could continue to make some money.

In fact, due to Leia's assistance, Umar was able to recuperate, maintain a basic flow of income, and return to work. For a man who helped support two teenage children and paid two thousand dollars in monthly rent for a house more than an hour away from Venice, the assistance was vital. Together, Leia's and Umar's actions did the work of granting Umar a type of informal sick leave. By working together to enhance each other's long-term profit, such interactions also indicate a sense of collective interests and behavior.

Khaled similarly needed some assistance. I walked onto the boardwalk one morning to the news that he had been arrested, the terms of which slowly unfolded over time and remained highly debated. Rumors indicated that a couple of vendors who were fed up with Khaled's level of informal authority decided to use what they thought was "a stack of priors" against him, leveling a minor charge against him that would get him wrapped up in the system. On one hand, this reiterates the extreme vulnerability of those working here, as well as the fickle nature of trust. On the other hand, even though people on the boardwalk did not fully understand the charges, I watched the otherwise invisible support structure kick into gear.

Soon after Khaled's arrest, a man I had never seen working here approached me, handing me Khaled's belongings—a small bag with his wallet, his identification, some clothes, and a couple of cell phones—to see if I could keep them safe. At the time, I had been working in more of an assisting role with Khaled. While he was in jail, two nearby merchants also located me to hand me letters he had sent. This allowed him to relay messages about watching over things in his absence. Interestingly, both Paul and I struggled to find information about Khaled's arrest during this time, since we became aware that none of us knew his legal name. The closest we ever came was in talking with Sheila, who had known him for years. "About ten years ago he got hit in the head real bad," Sheila told me. "And in his state of delusion, he told me his full name. I can't remember it, though." Eventually I checked his state-issued ID and found his official name to be nothing close to anything he went by on the boardwalk. Yet, however little people really knew of Khaled, it was because of their effort, and arguably my own, that he was able to seamlessly continue his work when he returned months later. If there had been a stack of priors, it did not seem to warrant the long-term sentence others had anticipated.

In the case of Umar and of Khaled, the expectations cultivated through ongoing interaction and exchange were mobilized in times of unanticipated emergency. In the midst of illness and arrest, both Umar and Khaled utilized social ties to maintain ongoing profit and preserve a symbolic presence on the block. This was a significant protection in a context with ongoing potential for turnover each day and competitors who might try to stake a claim. What shines through, particularly in the case of Khaled's arrest, is that social ties along the boardwalk were not rooted in acquiring any official knowledge of one another. There was little knowledge of names and addresses. Trust, after all, is not all encompassing, but emerges from the specific context of precariousness that many people face. The resulting community, however, can be extremely robust in the work it does to construct stability in an otherwise highly uncertain environment. And it is therefore vital to the subversive safety net.

These practices moved beyond meeting immediate needs and allowed for increasingly long-term benefits of social and economic stability. As individuals invested more resources, time, and effort, their own vulnerability also increased, allowing the potential for others to act in opportunistic ways for longer periods of time or to take advantage of one another's assistance by holding off on reciprocation. Yet, trust in the context of this uncertainty was able to garner even more significant results.

As we began to see in the previous chapter, block communities had gained—or more accurately, regained—primal importance following the lottery system. Blocks allowed for routinized interaction and moved from merely building expectations to interpreting and predicting one another's expectations. People invested in one another's long-term security, establishing a type of sick leave to ensure more durable economic stability. Through trust, participants garnered increasingly long-term results and built a community that could be mobilized in times of emergency. Moving beyond the mere one-on-one interaction that is task specific and immediate, here trust extended into a broader web of connected social ties to generate job stability. And being bound to the boardwalk meant people were rarely dependent on only one other person, but rather, were dependent on a web of people working together.

Defining the Contours of the Community

At 7 a.m., I walked up to the storefront, pulling my cart of merchandise and supplies. Manuel and Leia said hello as I placed my cart against the east-side storefronts. They told me I would be working in "that spot," and Manuel pointed to one of the spaces across the boardwalk, all of which were marked with empty cardboard boxes. Then they told me about an argument they'd had earlier that morning. "We came at five a.m.," they told me, "and had to fight that guy off." They continued, "He said he'd been working here all week; we told him it was full!"

This was the Saturday after I had met Kevin, who we met in the first section of this chapter, newly arrived from Miami with his ex-girlfriend and a cart of precious stones. Sure enough, Kevin was the man Manuel and Leia had "fought off." He had set up successfully on the block from Monday through Friday, during a particularly slow week when more than a few spaces were available for him to work. Though he had made direct requests with well-defined terms, once the weekend arrived, his time on the block was cut short by Manuel and Leia. They were protecting the community they had cultivated. Kevin had failed to appropriately read the boardwalk and understand that on this weekend—a lucrative time to sell—the boardwalk was no longer available to him.

As we saw in the previous chapter, the city had long desired open access of the boardwalk's western edge and had lamented the monopolization of spaces. But the permit program that had been the city's answer to issues of monopolization had merely shaped new forms of inequality around access. It prioritized different forms of capital, particularly for those with access to large social and kinship networks and those who had the financial means to invest in greater quantities of merchandise. The first-come-first-served policy was considered by many to be more equitable because it valued effort and seniority. It also put control back in the hands of smaller communities of people who could organize by block.

And so, on the Saturday morning when Kevin arrived to claim his space, Manuel and Leia drew clear boundaries around the established community of workers. Kevin quickly learned that he was on the outside. This interaction had the consequence of protecting the known set of participants on the block. After all, this was the very reason that Ricardo, as we saw earlier, could arrive with the assumption that he would have a spot for the day. While Kevin was lucky enough to get a direct response from Manuel and Leia (albeit not the one he had hoped for), other newcomers were made aware of their misreading through broader intimidation tactics.

One morning I sat with my back against the T-shirt shop, staring at the ocean and waiting for the setup time. Three long-haired Latino men wearing oversized T-shirts that might cue a typical hippie style, pulled a cart just south of me. They had stopped directly across from what was well established as Jaden's space. Jaden, a Black immigrant with a broad, muscular build who stood over six feet tall, was an extremely consistent presence. He also often used more than one space—a double-wide.

Over the years, he had adapted to whatever the regulation asked of him, often without missing a beat. For about six months, he had been setting up in the same two spaces, one of which was now under threat.

When Jaden came around the corner to see the three new-comers, he did not confront the men directly. Instead, he went across the boardwalk to his spot, picked up the piece of wood the men had placed there and dramatically threw it in the garbage. He yelled loudly, "You do not take my stuff!" into the air and walked away. Nobody went to talk with the men, nor did any-body confront Jaden. But the point was taken. The men gathered their belongings and moved into a section of concrete the city had deemed impermissible for vending and reserved for wheelchair access. Occupying this space was a finable offense, leaving the men vulnerable to punishment. In other words, they were pushed from a rightfully gained first-come-first-served space because in practice, spaces were rarely accessed on a first-come-first-served basis. This reiterates the point made earlier, that merely placing items on a space was not enough to ensure one's access. These men had not read the scene correctly and would therefore not find entry.

Notably, Jaden took an opportunity to reiterate his "owner-ship" over space by making a dramatic scene. He did not speak directly to the men, but rather informed everybody in the vicinity that this was "his" space, and he would reclaim it each morning. This was unsurprising to those of us who had been working near Jaden, but the "you're on your own" approach to newcomers could kick in at any moment. There was an understanding that things would right themselves—in other words, that breaches to the established order would meet some form of sanction. Newcom-ers were frequently on their own, indicating how the subversive safety net did not support all who entered this marketplace, but only those who wove it by making precarity work there each day.

In such an open space, where there were no formal barriers to participation, it was these practices that helped explain why the animal rights activist I once met could not seem to "find" a space from which to distribute informative pamphlets. It shed

light on why a University of Southern California art student I
met told me he had been trying, unsuccessfully, to get a spot for
over four years.

But was this merely an issue of competition for space? At a
place like the boardwalk, we might assume that these moments
of closure appeared only in relation to available space. However,
even when space itself was not at stake, people still demonstrated
a commitment to define and protect the limits of this community
of workers. In order for the subversive safety net to do supportive
work, it could not be made to catch every person who tried their
hand in this local economy.

After packing up my cart one night, I began to secure it with
a blue tarp and bungee cords. As I was making the final adjust-
ments, a man approached me. He was white, and likely in his
late thirties, though his skin had taken on a red, leathery quality
from repeated exposure to the sun. His brown hair was short and
messy, and he had nervous energy.

"Can I help you move your cart?" he asked, making a clear
effort to concentrate as he spoke.

"No, I'm OK," I responded.

"You don't need help?" he asked again.

At that moment Ricardo, who was working nearby, stood, and
walked over.

"Benson moves this cart," he said matter-of-factly.

Frustrated by the lack of available work, the man exclaimed,
"Oh, Benson moves every cart. He has this whole boardwalk!"

Ricardo seemed to want to end any back-and-forth, because
he responded quite aggressively, "Well, Benson moves this cart!"

The man walked away.

Given the prevalence of drug and alcohol use among groups
of tourists, transients, and a large population of folks who were
unhoused (a topic I turn to in the following chapter), there was
a constant flow of willing odd-job workers desiring quick cash.
Yet rather than accept services from the lowest bidder, Ricardo's
decision to interject and aggressively decline this man indicated
the importance of protecting already-established workers. Securing such jobs, therefore, was not always as easy as offering one's

services for a cheap fee. Here, Ricardo ensured the ongoing presence of Benson—a man with whom many of those working here maintained trust—further constructing a web of support.

The act of protecting Benson's job was a practice of defining the boundaries of a particular community—a community of workers. That is, while the cast of characters on the boardwalk may have been in constant flux, the boundaries of this community were only so porous. By defining outsiders, Ricardo, Leia, and Manuel also drew the boundaries around insiders, or "regulars." As they did, they shifted control over access into the hands of those already working here, limiting the availability of spaces for new arrivals. As workers here erected additional boundaries for newcomers, they constructed a collective threat, further building a communal experience to limit turnover and change. They protected the routinized interactions that fostered long-term benefits. This also revealed the way trust could contribute to exclusion and further marginalization of people who may already be vulnerable. Here, we begin to see the dark side of trust, that in protecting trust among known participants, workers created a closed community. But such closure could be an important mode of protection beyond the issue of competition for space and sales. In a place where people were constantly arriving and departing, where tourists and visitors poured in on weekends and hot summer days, where people tried their hand at living a bohemian lifestyle, people also learned to protect these boundaries in novel ways.

To many visitors, the boardwalk appeared a space of constant flux. Young backpackers arrived from around the country—their nights spent at nearby hostels or in sleeping bags on the grass, their days sitting, drinking, smoking, and socializing. They would often become linked to the local economy. Some people stayed longer and wanted to try their hand at selling goods or artwork. Some offered easy opportunities for drinking company. Some got into drugs and began a descent into the underbelly of boardwalk life. While the visitor may have seen a fluidity of people selling goods and hanging out on the boardwalk, there were clear boundaries.

"I'm Laura," I told a man standing with Ricardo one day.

"Doug," he said.

But Ricardo chimed in. "She's cool," he told Doug.

This made Doug laugh. "My name is Vince," he then said. "I thought you were part of the 'local chapter,'" he told me as he nodded his head in the direction of a group of young backpackers dressed in hoodies and various shades of military green and drinking on the grass. "I'm not going to go telling those guys my real name."

While Doug/Vince was rather quick to give up his air of mystery, his actions indicated a desire to interact differently with those he defined as insiders from those he defined as outsiders. Defining and protecting the boundaries of the community helped establish familiarity; people made sure that the expectations they had cultivated could reap benefits. Trust, then, became more robust. The seemingly chaotic flux that many visitors saw was mere background activity for a stable group of regulars.

Keeping newcomers and visitors at bay wasn't the only collective act necessary to define and protect the community. Workers also had to protect one another from threats that might arise—particularly the threats that arose from punitive approaches to public-space usage. For instance, Khaled reminded me to let people know if I saw the cops: "Even if nobody is doing anything wrong; it's good to know their patterns." Khaled was big on reading patterns.

Warning people of police presence was one way of dealing with the fact that cops were a wild card on the boardwalk. As we saw in chapter 1, Los Angeles Municipal Code 42.15 itself contained the kind of vague language that allowed discretionary enforcement to flourish. Some officers, like Campos and Harlow, established themselves as a regular presence. They also professed to police "the spirit of the law," and actively worked with people to construct the informal boundaries between permissible and impermissible behavior. But the Pacific Division also rotated officers on the ground; new cops, unfamiliar with such negotiations, posed new problems.

In addition, the ordinance was a living document. As discussed in the previous chapter, over the course of five years, LAMC 42.15

underwent major changes, causing even the most regular participants to enter new negotiations. And with each change, there
were always a slew of small infractions available to officers if they
wanted to use them. A table leg that extended beyond the borders
of a "designated space." An umbrella over four feet tall. A sun tent
erected on the grass. When the boardwalk gained official designation as a park, smoking a cigarette also became a finable offense.
As a result of the ever-changing regulations and discretionary
enforcement, the issue for workers became less about not doing
anything wrong and more about always knowing the whereabouts
of officers.

One day, Paul turned to me and said the cops were walking
up the boardwalk with video cameras to ask us questions. Sure
enough, a few police officers soon approached Paul's table and began to ask his name. Paul was particularly nervous because he
knew that the sale of jewelry had recently been banned from the
Free Speech Zone for having "more than nominal utility." He had
already begun painting, but he was still trying to offload his existing jewelry. And so, Paul claimed the jewelry was merely a "display." But the officers reiterated that such items were no longer
permissible to sell. In the end, they passed without issuing Paul a
ticket. After they walked away, though, I heard Paul on the phone.
"The cops are making their way up," he said. Afterward I asked
Paul if he had called Michelle, who was also trying to sell off her
inventory of jewelry. "Yes," he said, "I just called her."

Here we see how the boardwalk's linearity was a clear benefit for social interaction and support. Paul protected Michelle
from the economic shock that came with hefty fines. Paul thus
invested in the ongoing development of collective goals and positive expectations at the level of the community, from which he
would also benefit. Protecting trust thus took place as workers
provided unsolicited and proactive assistance, both demonstrat-
ing and fostering collective goals.

While Paul and Michelle both sold jewelry, data indicates
that it wasn't just their shared vulnerability around jewelry that
prompted action. For instance, one day Paul walked away to use
the bathroom. Upon noting a heavy police presence, he stayed

away from his table. In a flash, I saw Manuel run over to Paul's table and gather up necklaces, rings, and bracelets, sweeping them off into piles and putting them in one of Paul's nearby bins. "What's going on?" I asked, sensing his urgency. "The cops," he said. "Get rid of the jewelry."

As an artist, Manuel belonged to the group of workers who were regularly depicted in city regulation as "ideal" participants. As a result, he would likely never be in the same vulnerable position of Paul when it came to receiving fines for the sale of impermissible goods and merchandise. Yet while public debate often pitted artists against vendors, in everyday practice, these workers often joined forces. They developed a collective experience and aimed to shield one another from threats, even when artists and vendors did not share the same type of vulnerability. They acted in ways that constructed and protected the community—practices that continuously wove the subversive safety net.

Still, this portrait of community must consider the dynamic nature of social relationships. Over time, there were personal entanglements, breakups, and arguments. There were personality clashes and perceived nuisances. "Drama," as it was known, was inevitable. When Randy's style of hawking became frustrating for some, an argument ensued. Using credible threats of violence, Khaled "pushed" Randy to a new block. A long-term feud between Andrea and Barbara ended in Barbara getting "pushed" so far north that she ended up on the Santa Monica Pier. Two vendors were responsible for Khaled's incarceration of nearly a year. Emma moved to set up next to a new boyfriend until the relationship became physically abusive; after the breakup, she moved a few blocks north. Often, "drama" shifted over time, and the building of shared experiences over years often acted as glue within the community. Even Khaled, who partially blamed Hazel for his arrest, turned to me one day after his return. "I respect that she stayed," he said to me as the two continued to work on the same block. It was one more way that power dynamics remained fluid, and the strict sanctions we might find to maintain order in other informal economies rarely had purchase on the boardwalk.

Conclusion

I walked up to Leia while she sat on a folding chair against the inland wall, waiting for the 9 a.m. setup time. "Is your son coming today?" I asked.

"He's here," she said, lifting her hand up in a vague sweep of the space. "He's somewhere around here playing."

Leia's calm emerged in clear opposition to the narratives of chaos many visitors to the boardwalk expressed. Some spoke to me about their own discomfort and sense of vulnerability. One woman in her thirties told me she had been glad to have a companion on her run and emphatically clarified that she would never walk along the boardwalk on her own. Another man who had recently moved to the area with his wife told me of their shock during a morning stroll. "I was not expecting a scene from *The Walking Dead*," he said, referring to the popular television show about an apocalyptic world populated by deadly zombies. The police presence during the day often supported such narratives—a presence that multiplied at night as circling helicopters focused their searchlights on the pathway.

But Leia, a woman who participated in a practice of making precarity work each day, saw a subversive safety net otherwise invisible and inaccessible to those visitors. The kids were part of "the family," Khaled said to me. "They grow up here." Emma's then five-year-old son often whizzed by alone on his skateboard. The kids of a local merchant often ran outside to sit and paint with Randy. Michelle's seven-year-old son left her table and ran south to find Manuel's son. "They grow up differently too, really independent," Khaled said. It was more than being street smart, it was about learning how to communicate with a vastly diverse group of people—from billionaires to homeless folks, and people from all over the world. Khaled smiled with amusement and said that visitors always scrunched up their faces when they saw these young kids around, buying their own lunch. Visitors would ask, "Where are his parents?" But Khaled laughed and continued, "Just watch one of these tourist kids get lost, and they are just staring and afraid—they're scared of the people that want to help them. Parents now are scared; they hold their kids tight and say, *Don't talk to strangers*. The kids that grow up here can start a conversation with anybody."

The support that emerged around the children of those working here often illustrated the nature of role of the community that had formed here. One day, when I sat against Mr. Park's storefront, waiting during the early-morning hours. Manuel sat next to Leia in folding chairs, Paul on a stool. The calm suddenly broke with some commotion around the corner.

"*Se cayo! Se pego!*"

It was difficult to see who around the corner had sounded an alert, but Paul stood up immediately, and turned to Manuel. "He fell," he said.

Both men ran to the corner and disappeared around the building. A few minutes later, Paul returned calmly. "He fell and hit his head."

About ten minutes later, Manuel returned with his arm around his son, who was holding a bag of ice to his sullenly hung head.

Trust became quite robust on boardwalk, emergent in the everyday interactions people formed to rely on a set of fellow workers—people who provided vital stability in this form of precarious informal work. Manuel was aware of "the family," and used it as a vital resource when it was necessary to bring his son to work. It was one more way that the subversive safety net emerged as more than the sum of its parts.

In this chapter, I zoomed in on another aspect of making precarity work: the everyday interactions through which people cultivated a community of workers. It was this community that then served as another strand in the subversive safety net. Trust emerged as a key social mechanism in this process, one that is heavily shaped by the conditions of work on the boardwalk. It reared its head rather quickly, as people balanced a need to physically lay claim to space from which to work and a need to leave the space. It was cultivated over time through ongoing face-to-face interactions and exchanges, allowing people to build a set of expectations and then meet the expectations of others. The physical proximity of workers played an important role here, as did the consistency of the communities that formed on each block.

This, in fact, offers another window into the downfall of the Public Expression Participant Permit Program discussed in chapter 2. By reshuffling participants each week through the lottery draw, the permit program had arguably limited not only the development of trust, but the resources and stability that comes from that trust. The permit program had in many ways weakened the value of "the family." To stabilize the uncertainty and precariousness of the everyday, people worked to define the community through the exclusion of newcomers. Trust was not always on one's side; it also had a dark side.

The relationship of trust to community building also offered a window into the creation of a stable yet dynamic workplace. It offered a better understanding of the everyday interactions through which workers wove their safety net.[8] Over the years, I witnessed relationships gone bad, legal entanglements, prejudice. These issues, however, often served to shuffle people into new areas of the boardwalk rather than expel them altogether. In fact, people still had respect for participants who had, in their minds, wronged them in highly consequential ways. Showing up, day after day, was the sign of a commitment to "the family," even if you didn't like the person next to you.

In the next chapter, I expand on this notion of community. I show how making precarity work entails constructing compatibility between work and those behaviors often seen as incompatible with work. This practice allows the subversive safety net to emerge as a supportive structure built by (and accepting of) people whose needs are not being met by the standard safety net. Focusing on alcohol and drug use, I will show that as people produced an economic and social world capable of absorbing a diverse set of needs and experiences, they also produced a form of work that was shaped profoundly by those needs and experiences. The result is a social system replete with compatibilities and modes of support that are far too often overshadowed by a focus on abject poverty and overlooked for fear that they romanticize hardship. But rather than celebrating such "accomplishment," the very fact that so many people came together to manage these needs through participation in the marketplace deserves intense scrutiny. Power dynamics took particular form in this context, as some people became dependent on one another to get through the day. We must simultaneously be willing to examine how people assert a right to exist through the production of "work" while questioning the very circumstances that encourage this approach. The next chapter brings attention and understanding to this process while encouraging a critical lens that questions the very cracks in the system that have allowed this to occur in the first place.

4

Incorporating the Undesirable

Sal sat down next to me and began drinking a beer. It was just after 7 a.m. At the advice of Paul the night before, I had arrived early to secure a spot, and I'd been sitting on my stool against the closed storefronts for the previous thirty minutes. Paul and Ricardo had also come by to drop off a few items on the block, but they disappeared just as quickly. Now it was just me, Raúl, and Sal. A self-professed "OG" (the "original gangster" label proudly linked the neighborhood's history of gang activity), Sal had been pacing around in anxious anticipation of Ricardo's return. He wanted to unload Ricardo's tables and merchandise for some cash and was annoyed that Ricardo was sleeping off a party from the night before in his car. Sal told Raúl as much.

"Well, he's the boss," Raúl responded, seemingly unfazed by the situation.

Resigned to waiting, Sal now sipped his beer and began talking to me about women. "They're crazy" he said, "but I'm respectful." He told me he had almost gotten married once. "She made me choose between her and the beer," he said as he lifted the cup in his hand. "I chose the beer." He paused for a second and lowered his hand. "I wouldn't choose the beer again, though."

Sal's was not an uncommon situation. In fact, substance use was part and parcel of the varied—and often bumpy—life trajectories that had brought people together on the boardwalk. Similar to other urban settings that afford ongoing and relatively easy access to drugs and alcohol, the boardwalk could be understood as what the sociologist Jacob Avery has called an "enabling habitat."[1] As Khaled explained one morning, "Out here, people can't judge; everybody ends up here because of some issue. Family problems, addiction, they did something wrong, they're looking for themselves. They end up here because there is nowhere else to go." He lifted his hand toward the ocean: "This is the end." Or as Trey more pithily put it, "This is Venice, where the debris meets the sea."

But what does it mean to say there is "nowhere else to go" when clearly there are alternatives? Perhaps a more fruitful question is, how does a social world gain meaning as a "last somewhere"? And furthermore, what do social relations look like in a system where people managing a vast array of precarious circumstances may jokingly refer to one another as the "debris" caught and collected at the edge of the continent?

To answer these questions, this chapter turns to another way people make precarity work each day—by producing a social system inclusive of people whose needs, behaviors, and experiences are often ill suited to formal work arrangements. Such a production process then weaves yet another strand of the subversive safety net, catching those who believe they have nowhere else to turn. To show how this took place in the boardwalk marketplace, I zoom in on one manifestation of precariousness: those needs, behaviors, and experiences centered around drinking and drug use. As we will see, however, such practices can also become tightly bound with additional experiences of mental health problems and homelessness.

First, I describe three different relationships between substance use and work. Next, I show how these different relationships become interrelated parts of a social system, essentially producing a world in which various ways of drinking alcohol and using drugs become compatible with a local ecology of work. Such compatibility then disrupts many of the dominant moral constructions that condition access to work and worker status. I then turn more explicitly to the ways people embedded in this social system draw meaning from such interrelated practices, shining light on how the boardwalk in particular can become understood as a "last somewhere." Finally, I show how such a meaningful construction intersects with time and people's ongoing life trajectories, such that it becomes a supportive social world to which people can return or from which they can escape.

To be fair, my focus on the social and symbolic role of everyday drinking and drug use requires recognizing and tabling some dominant assumptions. First, the tendency to conflate substance *use* with substance *abuse* establishes a problem-oriented approach that limits the kinds of questions we ask and risks missing the way substance use gains meaning in people's lives.[2] Since the 1970s, research on the social and symbolic role of drugs and alcohol has been growing; anthropological and sociological accounts continue to illuminate the analytical potential of social and symbolic approaches to everyday drinking and drug use. People communicate and claim group membership through their choice of substances and their preferred methods for consuming or administering them.[3] People utilize substances to transgress, challenge, and reinforce gender distinctions and norms.[4] Substance use also brings new meaning to other behaviors—for instance, by excusing actions that were previously considered "unacceptable," such as violence and increased sexual freedom.[5]

Second, when we examine substance use alongside poverty and marginalization, it becomes heavily moralized—skewing analyses toward portraits of abject abuse and disorder through which people are made visible only as patients and clients. There is little room to view people as having agency, autonomy, and dignity, even if limited.[6]

Last, it is often the life conditions of marginalized workers that frame their drinking and drug use as pathology. We avoid the nuanced analyses reserved for artistic and creative individuals who may use drugs and alcohol for inspiration, or elite workers for whom networking events, company outings, and after-work social gatherings also center around drugs and alcohol. We gain greater insight into the nuanced ways that substance use becomes linked to the spheres in which they are most frequently constructed as being incompatible and problematic, particularly at work and in public.

For example, alcohol and drug use in public spaces is frequently viewed through the lens of disorder and consequently leads to punitive measures, but interactional research finds that both formal and informal control of substance use take place through more nuanced interactions and discretionary enforcement.[7] Evidence indicates that law enforcement officers often communicate subtle agreements of acceptance for "deviant" behavior,[8] and that the very people who discuss street drinking as being a morally offensive activity engage in more-complex negotiations on the ground to consider who, where, when, and how people are drinking.[9] Drinking practices in public parks and on sidewalks can also become ways for marginalized social groups to lay claim to spaces and places, assert identities, and access resources.[10]

Tabling many of the dominant assumptions around substance-use-as-abuse is by no means a call to ignore the health outcomes of harmful drinking and drug use, nor a romanticization of the challenging—and at times painful—circumstances and experiences that appear in this chapter and elsewhere in this book. As research has shown, the choices people make must be understood within the context of opportunities available. Choices may be rational, but this may also be understood as what the sociologists Eva Rosen and Sudhir Alladi Venkatesh call a "bounded rationality"—that is, people's pursuits become rational in the face of structural forces that marginalize them, and work that provides *"just enough"* may not be good, per se, but it "satisfices."[11] Without disregarding such realities, there is a similar opportunity in this case to shift the "social problems" lens and focus on understanding the way people themselves experience this form of work alongside other precarious life conditions.

Furthermore, by examining the emergence of a social system constructed precisely through the practices of people attempting to navigate everyday precarity, their strategies highlight the gaps in an ever-eroding standard safety net. Rather than left untouched by social service providers, many people here are caught in a web of services that impact their participation in the boardwalk's economy but do not offer a clear pathway out of it. As will become clear throughout the chapter, this is in part because people are not always convinced that service providers offer a better option than the subversive safety net they have woven for themselves.

As in every part of making precarity work, the neighborhood's identity as a site of counterculture shaped the way this practice played out, impacting the form the subversive safety net took as a result. Drinking and drug use remained a rather visible and celebrated part of Venice's social scene. The boardwalk itself was lined with bars and restaurants as well as medical marijuana dispensaries. Patrons sat outside these venues openly drinking alcohol, legitimated by the flimsy stretch of rope or plexiglass panel that delineated private patrons from public drunks. As we saw in the first chapter's opening description of the boardwalk, the young workers in green scrubs who called to passing visitors to "get legal" often lent an air of amusement to the medical marijuana dispensaries. Liquor stores dotted the boardwalk, and food kiosks capitalized on the need to conceal open containers of alcohol by selling their paper and Styrofoam cups for twenty-five cents.

In such a context, we might assume a free-for-all to unfold, but this would gloss over the complicated ways that drinking and drug use become bound up with this social and economic world. Furthermore, it fails to recognize the limits of the subversive safety net, which is not all encompassing. For one, drinking alcohol, smoking marijuana, and using other drugs were not sanctioned public activities. Furthermore, once the boardwalk received its designation as a city park, even cigarette smoking was restricted, making the act of smoking any substance more vulnerable to surveillance. As a result, drinking and drug use here became tied to social relations in more nuanced ways.

Bringing Substance Use to Work (and Work to Substance Use)

Much of what we know about the drinking habits and drug use among street-level entrepreneurs still reproduces portraits of incompatibility, particularly as people recede into the hidden corners of urban American to get their fix.[12] In part, this is because the very marginalization that pushes people to earn income in urban public spaces also hinders their ability to engage in substance use on site. As a public space, the boardwalk offered entrance into an economy with few formal barriers. It was therefore shaped by the life conditions of people who required such ease of access. People brought varied substance-use practices to work.

In what follows, I describe how drinking and drug use become meaningful ways to take a break from work, construct a cycle between substance use and work, and define the limits of compatibility. The three examples I give, while not exhaustive accounts of all the ways people drank alcohol and used drugs on the boardwalk, reflect dominant ways people linked their substance use to work.

Taking a Break

Ricardo stood behind the folding table full of leather bracelets and accessories; his head was down in apparent concentration. While most days he worked alone, a few of Ricardo's friends had joined him on this day. They brought folding chairs and stashed a couple six packs of beer under the table, an area concealed by the cloth hanging over the table's front and sides. They sat behind Ricardo talking and joking with one another, sipping beer from Styrofoam and paper soda cups they had purchased from the food kiosks. Every now and then, they squatted down to refill their cups from under the table.

Ricardo stood at his display table with his back to his friends, working a needle and thread through the end of a leather strap likely to become a bracelet. Having worked in the space next to him for weeks, I could see his characteristic stoicism lighten with the social scene that developed around their drinking. As a group of people passed in front of his table, he said flatly, "*Si pasas sin comprar, sigue pasando* [If you walk by without buying anything, keep on walking]." Then he turned to his friends and me with a smirk and a chuckle, transforming the nonsale into a shared moment of humor.

Throughout the day, Ricardo moved between working and drinking from the stash of beer under the table. By late afternoon, he and his friends had become increasingly social, laughing and talking together about salsa dancing and women. Ricardo walked to the edge of his space and slowly began to move his body to the music playing from the speakers of the store across the pathway. "This is my favorite," he said as he raised and dropped his arms in perfect synchronicity with the beat. Without cracking a smile, he mimicked an interpretation of a tribal powwow dance. His friends laughed loudly in encouragement, as Ricardo danced with a look of thoughtful determination.

One of the hardest-working vendors on the boardwalk, Ricardo appeared to enjoy participating in a break from the monotony of work on the boardwalk. In fact, it is the very monotony of this workplace that Ricardo used as a tool to entertain his friends. The beat to which Ricardo danced in such synchronicity played on an unforgiving loop from the speaker across the pathway—all day, every day—allowing him an intimate and almost carnal knowledge of the rhythm.

For Ricardo and his friends, drinking alcohol became a social act that allowed for moments of levity and humor during the workday. In a space that was unforgiving in its constant surveillance and lack of privacy, such moments among friends became increasingly valued. Furthermore, leisure was not so easily delineated on the boardwalk, since the workday extended into evenings and weekends. It was not uncommon for workers to break such monotony with meaningful interruptions, what the sociologist Donald Roy famously called "banana time."[13] On the boardwalk, leisure was socially produced rather than delineated by space and time, and drugs and alcohol played a key role in that production. Ricardo took from the surrounding environment—including the passing public and repetitive music—to produce a humorous subject for his enjoyment and that of his friends. His friends provided a necessary audience, drawn together by the shared activity of drinking alcohol.

This was further evidenced when Ricardo arrived late—after 12 noon—to his space and in a rather jovial mood. He carried a bag of beers with him and put them under one of the tables. His

friends Roberto and Enrique joined him behind his tables, and the
three men shared the beers by pouring them into Styrofoam cups.
The men appeared to be having a good time as they spoke mostly
in Spanish, again returning to their common discussion of dancing and women. Ricardo turned to me and told me he had arrived
at the boardwalk late and was therefore "not worried about working" this particular day. Instead, he told me he would work the
next day. I noticed that his tables were almost bare, but since he
was not actively unpacking any additional items, I asked him if
his goods were set up yet. "Yes," he said, adding that the weekend
had been "really good" for him.

Khaled similarly used marijuana to take some time to himself.
He would set up his tables, cover them in a cloth that hung down
to the ground in front, light a joint, and sit in the "private" space
created by the tables and cloth. Such moments often allowed him
a chance to calm down, be alone, and take a break.

Many workers in the formal economy, even those precariously
employed, do not spend their days off at their workplace. But as
we learned in prior chapters, the boardwalk's marketplace is an
ephemeral worksite that required ongoing investment in its production. Workers' physical presence was often key to maintaining
access. The precarious nature of the work, shaped both Ricardo
and Khaled's production of leisure.

Maintaining a Cycle

It was a beautiful morning—the sky was clear, the air clean and
crisp, the ocean a perfect strip of dark blue against the horizon.
Three carts loaded with goods sat at the edge of the boardwalk. In
front of the coffee shop, groups of people were chatting about the
time change, as daylight savings time had just ended.

At the end of the block, Emma stood with her young son in
tow, talking with Mark, Khaled, and Benson.

"How's it going?" I asked them all as I approached.

Mark smiled. "All set up," he said, pointing to the cart he had
placed across from his usual space a few blocks north.

I peeked on the boardwalk and saw a vibrant scene in the making. The eastern edge was dotted by carts, each piled high with merchandise and covered in tarps. Rennie and a crew of people I didn't all recognize stirred under the scaffolding. Among them were piles of blankets, tarps, pillows, bags, and a couple of old office chairs—a disheveled arrangement in direct contrast to the neatly packed carts.

Benson turned to me. "Do you know what time it is—with this change and all?"

I grabbed my phone, recognizing the ease a smartphone offered in adjusting to daylight savings. "Eight fifty-eight. You've got two minutes."

"Thanks," he said, and walked away.

Benson approached one cart sitting against the storefronts on the east side and began to push it across the pathway. He then returned for the next cart, pulling it into the space along the western edge. Then the third cart.

Khaled and I soon moved to the western edge and watched as Benson worked, transferring carts from the east side to the west side. "He moves quickly," I said.

Khaled laughed. "And he's so little," he said, pointing to the fact that Benson stood at about five-foot-two. "Benson is the man out here," Khaled added. "He does work for everybody, and everybody knows it."

As mentioned in chapter 3, Benson was one of the most dependable and consequential odd-job workers I met on the boardwalk. Vendors, artists, and performers paid him cash to move their items to and from a storage unit each morning and evening. He swept nearby sidewalks for businesses. He watched over stores at night. Benson's actions greatly informed my own ability, and that of others, to accurately read the scene. His placement of carts along the east side foretold of the specific social arrangement to expect during the upcoming workday, something he typically confirmed at the end of each previous day. So, if a cart sat unpacked all day, it often communicated an unexpected absence—maybe a late arrival or an early departure. It was Benson's work that communicated to others an underlying social meaning of the seemingly mundane boardwalk scene.

But Benson's immense dependability could not be disconnected from the challenges he faced in being unhoused and underemployed and engaging in regular drug use. During the years I lived in Venice, Benson slept in a small store on the east side of the boardwalk. The structure itself was more of a kiosk, with three solid walls and a rolling garage door with a sliding gate out front. Margaret, a white woman in her forties, rented the store to sell trinkets and tourist memorabilia. In addition, she charged a group of vendors a monthly fee for the right to store their belongings there at night. So long as Benson moved the carts in after Margaret had closed and out before she needed to open, she allowed Benson to sleep there as well. And while she and many of the vendors relied on Benson in vital ways, they also all acknowledged that Benson engaged in regular drug use.

I turned to Paul while working and told him Benson had requested an advance on his fee for moving and storing the cart. I was still new to the game of working on my own, so I wanted to check with Paul to verify if this was normal.

"He probably just wanted to get high," Paul said matter-of-factly.

Another time, Khaled also added to the portrait of Benson's drug use by assuring me that for all his hard work, Benson "took care of himself." He said, "He has a crack problem," but added that it was just Benson's "thing." He reiterated: "Out here you can't judge. You just let people be people."

Benson's drug use still allowed him to complete his jobs, and—for good or bad—people who depended on him were largely unbothered by it. His role became possible specifically because a set of needs emerged from the precarious nature of work on the boardwalk. Vendors, artists, and performers were required to set up their goods and merchandise in first-come-first-served spaces along the western edge of the boardwalk. Consequently, they had to locate daily parking spaces or leave cars parked illegally while they unloaded. They had to carry bins and boxes from cars and storage units, roll carts piled high with merchandise, tables, fabric, and umbrellas, and sweep sand to clear spaces from a night of heavy wind. They had to unpack bins in the morning and pack them up again at night. For people with enough cash on hand, it was possible—and often necessary—to pay others to assist with these daily tasks. It was not uncommon for these support roles to be filled by people managing substance use and dependency issues.[14]

Benson and other odd-job workers often entered a cycle of working for cash, getting drunk or high, and then working for more cash. Such behavior is often examined through the lens of poverty, addiction, or abuse, but approaching Benson as a worker allows us to consider, as the anthropologist Kathleen Millar has argued, those "forms of living" so often equated with deprivation.[15] Benson built important relationships and put a great deal of energy into his work on the boardwalk. He dedicated himself to hobbies, particularly architectural design, and acquired a laptop and computer-aided design (CAD) software that was once stolen from him—and more important, returned to him. He constructed his own time off during the height of other people's workday, when I would find him researching, reading, or using his design software. Watching Benson over the years, I could see that his drug use and his work operated as mutually constitutive life practices. Essentially, Benson was always blurring the lines between work and substance use, as both practices informed each other and gave them meaning.

Undermining the Boundary between "Work" and "Vagrancy"

Rennie walked toward me holding a guitar in one hand and a cigarette in the other. "Hi!" he said.

Aware that Rennie slept in a nearby alley, I was concerned that the previous night's rain and temperature dip would have been difficult. So, I asked him how he had gotten through the night.

"I'm trashed already," he responded with unconvincing enthusiasm.

He asked me to hold his guitar while he used both hands to shield his cigarette and match from the air. The wood of his instrument was rough and beaten, but the strings all seemed intact.

Rennie often held cardboard signs soliciting money from tourists and visitors. They displayed humorous statements like OUT OF WORK SUPERMODEL and NEED A COLD FUCKEN' BEER. He also sold the signs themselves to amused tourists. When we stood by the coffee shop in the morning before his workday began, Rennie lamented having to "go to work," adding frustratedly that the cops never seemed to understand this. Law enforcement officers often scolded him for sleeping on the sidewalk or illicitly holding spaces for other vendors, insinuating or stating directly that he was *really* just hanging around to drink. "I'm working!" he'd tell me in response to the doubts of law enforcement.

And as evidence, Rennie's sales operation became more "legit," as he put it, over time. He talked about investing in the job to improve his signs. Most specifically, he located new cardboard, discarded markers, and crayons to increase the color variation and improve the writing. Perhaps his biggest shift was when he made a sign advertising his signs. It stated BUM SIGNS, and stipulated a price of two dollars per sign and one dollar for a photo of the signs. There were clear benefits to this marketing endeavor. "Some Australians came by and gave me fifteen dollars for four!" he once told me excitedly. "Fifteen is great, considering they are two dollars a sign."

By deciding to remain stationary in one of the marketplace's designated spaces and sell the signs typically used to solicit donations, Rennie converted solicitation into art vending. But his relationship between work and drinking also defined the limits of compatibility and pushed the capacity of the subversive safety net: Rennie's stable location and expanding business began to attract larger groups of people interested in pooling money for alcohol.

I spoke with Rennie after watching him place a large bottle of what appeared to be tequila underneath a blanket. I asked him about the signs he was making. "That's the art department," he told me as he pointed to the small tent on the grass behind him. A woman emerged from the tent, holding up her jeans with one hand so they would not fall from her waist. But the "art department" would work to define, and illuminate, the limits of support in this social system. Rennie was able to earn cash, and his signs were often a hit with tourists eager to purchase a bit of Venice's off-beat counterculture. But the activity drew a group of people with similar goals of purchasing alcohol, linking Rennie to people (and social problems) that veered from counterculture into problematic public intoxication, drug use, and homelessness. It was this visible link that led to Rennie's increased vulnerability to state surveillance.

For instance, one evening, while most workers were beginning to dismantle their work areas and pile things up for the day, Rennie sat on the grass drinking from a Gatorade bottle, a small group of people scattered on blankets and folding chairs surrounding him. Two LAPD officers passed by on their Segways. One stopped, walked up to Rennie, and said, "Give me that bottle." She smelled it and told him to leave the area or she would arrest him. She said, "You saw me and still drank from it anyway, so now *everybody* needs to get out of here." The group of people stood and started to move the folding chairs off the grass.

While Rennie had quite clearly committed an open-container violation, police generally tolerated concealed drinking in front of them. For instance, I never witnessed Ricardo receive a ticket for substance use; nor did Khaled's ongoing marijuana use end in such state control. Indeed, the officer's statement was not that Rennie should not have been drinking, but that he should have stopped when he saw her. The subversive safety net may be robust, but the support is not all encompassing. There is a tacit agreement between law enforcement officers and those working in the marketplace, much of which hinges on one's ongoing commitment to make it work. By failing to remain in this gray area, Rennie was no longer blurring a line between "work" and "vagrancy"—he was crossing it. The disrespect was not merely in his drinking, but in *seeing* her *see* him, and continuing to drink anyway. Not only was crossing this line consequential to Rennie, but it labeled an entire group of people as problematic and no longer deserving of the right to claim space for themselves.

Becoming a Social System

Up to this point, I have laid out three different ways that people combine drinking, drug use, and work on the boardwalk. For people like Ricardo, bringing alcohol to work allowed them to produce some leisure. In the case of Benson, we saw how drug use and work became mutually constitutive practices, informing each other and intricately intertwined. Rennie's practices show how people construct work around their ongoing substance use, reaching and defining the limits of compatible practices in the boardwalk's marketplace. While each of these relationships played out in a broader social scene and gained meaning through people's social relations, I turn now to examine more explicitly the way such practices became interrelated parts of a social system, bringing the subversive safety net—and its limits—into focus.

Though drinking and drug use are often understood and analyzed as individual practices, they also gain social meaning. Furthermore, in a public workplace like the boardwalk and among people for whom private spaces may be lacking, many of these practices ripple through the social world. People on the boardwalk developed a rather intimate understanding of one another's reaction to alcohol or drugs. Such understandings informed their relationships and notions of relative vulnerability.

For example, when Khaled and I stood behind the table when Chuck approached us, standing and staring half at us and half into space.

Khaled laughed a little. "Do you know where you are right now?" he asked Chuck. "Do you know who you're talking to?"

Chuck seemed to hear Khaled, but he just looked beyond us and made his way toward the grassy mound behind our space.

"He's perpetually out of it," Khaled said. "It takes him a long time to process."

Like Benson, Chuck was a regular odd-job worker on the boardwalk. Vendors like Ricardo and Paul frequently paid him to complete small, urgent tasks. Chuck was a white man, tall and lean, with messy blond hair and that blank look on his face; I would not be surprised if he managed some mental health issues, though I cannot know for certain. What is certain, however, is that he drank alcohol throughout the day, and those who hired him were aware of this practice. In fact, this became one consideration of many when hiring people to perform necessary tasks.

When Chuck walked by me and Ricardo on his way toward the grass that separates the boardwalk and the sand, Ricardo turned to tell me that Chuck had always been calm and that he didn't really start any "trouble." Ricardo went on to say that Chuck was a really "good guy." When Chuck was drunk, he consistently "passe[d] out" on the grass. He was pretty "even," Ricardo said—a quality much in demand on the boardwalk. And so, it was not just Chuck's availability for immediate odd jobs that made him a part of the social ecology of work, but also his distinct response to alcohol. Since he was frequently passed out on the grass, he avoided arguments. And since tourists were also scattered on the grass to sunbathe, he did not draw attention. As the sociologist Andrew Deener has argued, the boardwalk's bohemian identity veiled some of the homelessness, mental health problems, and addiction issues since these behaviors not only mingled with the sanctioned substance use offered by the bars, restaurants, and marijuana dispensaries, but tinged the scene with a degree of seemingly authentic counterculture and grit.[16]

While Chuck may have spent the cash he earned on alcohol, his ongoing availability, need for cash, and calm response to drinking alcohol made him an acceptable—even vital—participant in the boardwalk's economy. Chuck's role in the local economy and his daily behavior at work became understood through his alcohol use. Still, Chuck could easily become wrapped up in relationships that brought him closer to the limits of compatibility.

As described earlier, Rennie's way of drinking and working clearly defined the limits of compatibility by exceeding them. But his actions still gained meaning within a set of social relations on the boardwalk—that is, his behavior became part of a social system by sparking the exclusion of people not engaged in an everyday practice of making precarity work and by diverting police attention away from people who might be taking a break or maintaining a cycle.

I once saw Rennie and Chuck in the back seat of a parked LAPD sedan. Chuck appeared to be laughing.

Khaled turned to me. "They'll be out tomorrow," he said.

Soon afterward, Harold strode by. "They took both of them," he said. He seemed amused, smirking while he spoke. He told us that the cops had wanted to take him as well, but he had declared, "I'm not going." He smiled and said lightheartedly, "Rennie and I flipped a coin," implying the arrest was determined by the outcome of this coin toss.

Feeding off Harold's amusement, we laughed, and Khaled added that things had become "ridiculous."

As was often the case for drinking or sleeping in public, Rennie was arrested and spent a few days in jail before returning directly to the boardwalk.

Quite different from Rennie, Harold, and even Chuck for that matter, Khaled believed himself to have the freedom to engage in substance use as he pleased. He said directly that he could "smoke [marijuana] or whatever, because those [other] guys are magnets [for police]." He went on, "You could be right here smoking, and they [the police] won't even see you. They'll be looking over you at those guys." And Khaled had at least some evidence of this.

When I asked Khaled about his relationship with local police officers, he told me he and "the stocky brunette" officer were "cool." He said that when he was "smoking a bong" recently, the same officer had passed by and called out, "You're going to make it so obvious?" He had simply smiled and yelled back to her, "It's not pot!" He then reiterated that having faced no consequences for such behavior, he and the officer were "cool."

Not only did this type of discretionary enforcement shape the way substance use gained meaning alongside work, but it shaped the meaning and nature of social relations on the boardwalk. Participants like Paul, Ricardo, and Khaled often offered some stability to Rennie's participation, ensuring that he could remain tied to the economy. For instance, when Rennie, Chuck, and Tiny all decided to spend a day at a nearby barbecue, it was Paul and Ricardo who made sure to protect Rennie's space.

Taking on the type of informal management over block spaces that we learned about in the previous chapter, the men allowed a performer on the space who they believed would be there for just one day. This way, nobody could make any inroads. In a similar fashion, Khaled told me one day that he had preferred to move to a different spot on the block but didn't want to "step on Rennie's toes."

I have every reason to believe that people genuinely wished the best for Rennie, but protecting Rennie was not merely altruism. As Khaled mentioned, Rennie served as a distraction to the police who gave people like Ricardo and Khaled a bit more wiggle room to engage in their own substance-use practices in public. With Rennie serving as a "magnet" for police attention, Khaled had a better chance of getting away with more.

People learn the kind of logic that officers apply when policing public spaces and activities—even as it diverges from strict application of law as written—and apply it to mitigate their own vulnerability to law enforcement. Applying such wisdom, or what the sociologist Forrest Stuart has called becoming "copwise," may also encourage people to police themselves, aware that certain activities (or scenes) draw different levels of attention.[17]

On the boardwalk, workers who may not even engage in any type of substance use themselves still applied this knowledge to protect the broader community of workers. When a woman holding a garbage bag and visibly reacting to some sort of amphetamine approached Andrea about assisting her, Andrea told her to leave immediately. "That's not how it works here!" she exclaimed. When a group of young boys approached Ricardo asking for drugs, he responded in a low and mumbled speech until the boys became so frustrated, they walked away. When an undiscerning tourist popped open a beer on the grass behind Umar's stand, Umar walked over and told the man he had better conceal it. There were many ways the compatibility between substance use and work necessitated investment, and both law enforcement as well as workers themselves participated in defining these limits.

Becoming the "Last Somewhere"

In a conventional society fixated on the virtue of work, the dominant assumption is that a "good" worker is a sober one. This underpins legislation to ensure a "drug-free workplace" and supports the right of employers to widely administer pre- and post-employment drug screening.[18] Here we find a social system where people can work without adhering to such strict notions of recovery and sobriety, even if that work exploits their very needs. I now turn to the ways that social system becomes a place to decenter stigmatized identities, offer and locate support, and adopt dignified pathways forward, even if some cases should be understood in a context of severe constraint. In becoming such a place, the boardwalk also takes on an important role in people's life trajectories, being that "somewhere" to which they can return or from which they can escape.

As I discussed in prior chapters, Tim was a relatively well-resourced vendor, recently divorced and unemployed. He frequently employed Chuck and RJ to work on commission or perform odd jobs. As we saw in chapter 2, RJ worked side by side with Tim during the permit program as a kind of sales partner. RJ rotated between sleeping in the street, a storage unit, and occasionally the church-run shelter. However, his nighttime drinking left him in a state of agitation most mornings, irritable and unable to find his array of belongings, from clothing to cigarettes. The morning's aggravated search was almost always dramatized by the fact that RJ's choice of clothing was a large fishing vest replete with a multitude of pockets.

Tim had relationships with both Chuck and RJ that he framed in terms beyond employment. For instance, Tim told me he had given Chuck housing, which he later clarified to mean a table for shelter and a yoga mat to sleep on. Time told me that with the addition of stuffed animals and blankets he provided, Chuck had a basic shelter on the boardwalk at night. Tim said he fed and paid Chuck in the morning and that he was planning to "get [Chuck] off that [drinking]." He added, "And RJ too!"

Though Tim was not a habitual drinker himself, he drew on the drinking practices of men like Chuck and RJ to structure his work relationships and frame his own sense of purpose on the boardwalk. In committee meetings of the neighborhood council, he frequently advocated for greater representation of the boardwalk's large homeless population, many of whom managed alcohol or drug dependency. As discussed in chapter 2, this relationship was mutually beneficial to a degree, as Tim frequently provided RJ with rides to local city council meetings or to purchase merchandise in downtown Los Angeles. But RJ often complained that Tim failed to follow through on promises and encroached on RJ's market by selling similar items. Tim, however, expressed a sense of accomplishment and pride—however paternalistic—that he was assisting RJ.

In this way, substance use played a role in decentering stigmatized identities for both men. It was through Tim that RJ and Chuck were able access the capital necessary to work, including merchandise, folding tables, and space. RJ became Tim's most consistent "partner," and he took pride in his ability to build a "business." But Tim also took pride in his role as a mentor and provider for RJ, and rather than see himself as "unemployed," he framed himself as an advocate and activist for the rights of "the homeless." At one point, he went so far as to make a website and run (unsuccessfully) for city council.

When Rennie and his BUM SIGNS were featured in a national news article that exposed the challenges of policing the boundaries of "art," he could hardly contain his excitement in sharing it with me. As I read the article, I saw that the journalist had clearly centered Rennie's identity around his homelessness, but the article itself was not about homelessness or addiction—it was about the agency and innovation of people living on the street who had learned how to confuse the LAPD by playing with the meaning of art. In the article's descriptions, Rennie was also an active contributor to an economic and social scene. And he clearly valued that article: whenever the clipping went missing or got wet from rain, which was often, he asked me if I could reprint it, which I did, or if I had access to a laminator, which I did not.

Through the stories of Rennie and many others who sold goods and services in the boardwalk's public marketplace, we witness people taking the opportunity to establish their own autonomy and dignity. Many directly counterposed their own strategies to manage their precarious position with the alternative of taking from others. Instead, they saw their economic activities as actively contributing to an important economic and social world, and they used the boardwalk marketplace as a space for building an independent path forward.

As we have seen and will see again, such agential action—particularly as it played out within a web of complex social relations—did not always lead to objectively positive results. Sal, who we met at the beginning of the chapter as he sat drinking a beer, was normally a gregarious odd-job worker with loud cackling laugh and bounding step. But one day I saw him hunched over, his face pale. He approached Raúl and me. Raúl took a quick look at him and must have surmised the situation, because he immediately asked him if he needed a drink. Sal told him that none of the stores were open yet except for one on Washington, a main avenue about a mile south. Raúl stepped off the bike he had been straddling and handed it over to Sal. He told him to go grab something to drink. When Sal pedaled away, Raúl turned to me and said, "I know how it feels."

Raúl's own experience with alcohol dependency prompted him to provide Sal with the resources necessary to continue drinking. His action played an important role in maintaining Sal's relationship between alcohol consumption and work. Options to earn income while avoiding the symptoms of withdrawal are rare, particularly beyond the more hidden spaces of the informal and often illicit economy. This support—albeit subjectively defined—not only was a way to meet Sal's needs in their current form, but also allowed his ongoing presence and availability for odd-job work. Without Raúl's intervention, it is quite possible Sal would have been too sick to work. Instead, Raúl ensured that vendors and artists like Ricardo and Paul could continue to access Sal's labor.

But Raúl too had his challenges, shaped largely by the way he interpreted his own choices. He approached me early one morning and reminded me that it was Cinco de Mayo. "The day we fucked the French," he said, laughing. (In this case, "we" meant Mexicans, as the event commemorates the Mexican army's victory over colonizing French forces in 1862.) "People are probably going to be drunk," he told me. Unprompted, Raúl placed himself in opposition to the "drunk" people who would celebrate the day and told me that he was enjoying being sober. As we learned of Raúl in chapter 2, he had come back to the boardwalk after what he called "bottoming out." Upon his return, he was working with his "*primos*," or cousins, who had agreed to help him get started again by providing space and some goods to begin selling. So far, so good, he told me—though there were clear drawbacks to sobriety as well. "Sleeping is harder. I can't handle people as much. They just want to talk so much," he told me. "When you drink, you just want to talk and talk. And now I'm like, Hey man! I'm tired and I want to sleep. But they keep going." He imitated his companion: "But man, man, listen . . ."

Zephyr and his dog joined us on the bike path, and the two men exchanged greetings and discussed the impending rain. When Zephyr left, Raúl told me that he was "another one," going on to explain that he too was a person with a wealthy family who chose to live in his van rather than ask his family for support. Drawing parallels to himself, Raúl said Zephyr did not want to take handouts from people. Raúl said his own cousin did not understand why he would choose to sleep in street rather than stay with family or borrow some money. Raúl explained to me that he did not see this as an option. "That is *their* money, not mine," he said firmly. He said he would consider sleeping in his cousin's friend's tattoo shop—something his cousin was trying to arrange—only during the colder weather. "Right now it's not so bad, but come winter, it'll be worse," he said.

Raúl clearly rejected the idea of a "handout," defined in terms of assistance with housing or money. Instead, he accepted his cousins' help to access the opportunity to work, because the work was honest and offered an independent way forward. Similar to other cases in which people construct their own meanings of decency, this allowed Raúl to access what he perceived to be a dignified identity, framed through his decision to do the right thing.[19] But it also meant there were constant challenges to his sobriety that he might not have experienced if he had slept indoors. Here we can see that Raúl drew on a particular brand of US-promulgated neoliberal ideology that frames monetary assistance as a shameful "handout" and the opportunity to work as honorable. In his case, however, this framing encouraged him to accept circumstances that made staying sober more difficult. People tried their best to manage precarious life conditions through "dignified" strategies that rejected assistance, and thus could exacerbate those very conditions. It was a counterintuitive consequence of the "bootstrap" mentality.[20]

Identity projects and forms of support emerged and played out in different ways for different participants in the boardwalk economy. Tim's identity was closely tied to his understanding of support for RJ and Chuck, developing an understanding of himself as a worker-activist. Rennie constructed his work as meaningful because it played an important role in blurring the definition of art in this quirky economy, as well as any distinctions between being homeless and being a worker. Sal garnered important support that he would not likely have received in other workplaces—the support to meet his immediate needs and avoid withdrawal. Raúl took it upon himself to keep men like Sal going, but he understood his own decision to work his way up from "bottoming up" in direct opposition to accepting "handouts." People here carved out a place for themselves, a kind of last somewhere. The boardwalk, in becoming such a place, played an important role in people's life trajectories. It became somewhere to which they could return or from which they could escape.

The Pull of the Boardwalk

"Laura!" I heard my name called and turned around to see Benson standing on the corner.

"How's it going?" I asked.

"Fine." He told me. "I've got an appointment today."

I thought I should not pry. People rarely wanted to discuss their "appointments." I continued to the coffee shop but returned to Benson on my way back. I noticed he was carrying a book on architecture and what appeared to be a day planner.

"I'm waiting for my psychiatrist," he told me. Then he clarified, "My social worker is coming to take me." He went on to tell
me that his social worker believed he was suffering from "severe
depression" and "delusions." "They told me I'm hallucinating,"
he said. But he said that although he himself believed he was de-
pressed, he was much less convinced about the hallucinations. He
explained that, as he understood it, his social worker had framed
the diagnosis as a resource. "She said I could get SSI [Social Security disability payments] . . . so I can play crazy if I need to." He
said that the "Nazis" at the Social Security office could "decide if
I'm crazy or not."

Before we could continue the conversation any further, a white
van pulled up on Speedway and stopped at the end of the block.
Two young women sat in the front seats, both of whom appeared
white and in their twenties. Benson walked up to the van, slid the
back door open, and got in.

While characterizing the role these social workers played in
Benson's life as positive or negative is difficult, it is a noteworthy
example of how Benson's attachment to the boardwalk left him
both available for—and vulnerable to—medical attention and social services. He was far from the only member of the community
I met who seemed to openly doubt their diagnoses and communicated a choice to use them to access necessary care; the veracity
of medical diagnoses is therefore beyond the scope of this book.
However, people believed neurocognitive disorders offered them
access to support through the standard safety net. This support
became one of the many ways people pulled from a patchwork of
uncoordinated federal and state assistance programs to continue
their work lives on the boardwalk, rather than find alternatives to
it. In this way, it becomes clear that the boardwalk economy had
gained meaning beyond mere survival, as people returned to the
boardwalk even when other basic needs were met.

In fact, Benson eventually received housing and moved out
of the store. I moved away around the same time, relocating a
two-hour drive inland. Nearly two years following that initial
"appointment" with the social workers, I caught up with Benson
again.

"How are you doing?" I said.

"Good," he said. "I got off the street. I have a place on Vernon [a large avenue in South Los Angeles]. It's the 'hood. Real rough," he told me with more than a little concern in his face.

"You still working out here, though?" I asked, realizing that this new housing put him about twenty miles away, which, considering the bus route through Los Angeles traffic, easily made the trip over an hour.

"Yeah, I'm still coming to work," he said, smiling. Then he reiterated: "It's rough over there."

Benson indicated that work—at least, the way he constructed it on the boardwalk—played an important role in his life. His return to the boardwalk after securing housing also indicated that this role went beyond a mere need to "survive," or working in exchange for a place to sleep in the storage unit. If Benson had merely been engaging in survival strategies, as implied in much of the literature on homelessness and poverty, he would have likely adapted to opportunities closer to home. Instead, he continued "coming to work" even when doing so required more effort and was no longer socially and economically tied to his living arrangement. Whatever support SSI provided him, his behavior indicated that it did not replace the supportive social world of the subversive safety net.

In her 2018 account of garbage recyclers on the outskirts of Rio de Janeiro, Kathleen Millar exposed the draw of the dump—a draw often overlooked by scholars and policymakers seeking to make sense of seemingly destitute decisions to work among filth. It is in understanding this ongoing return to the dump that Millar began to better understand the decisions workers make each day to manage the precariousness of their life conditions.[21] In the case of Benson, it does not appear that he was waiting to find a way out of his work role. Instead, the boardwalk was something to which he returned.

But while Benson still valued returning to the boardwalk, others were happy to put it in their past. In chapter 3, I introduced Jorge, a man in his fifties who often came to the boardwalk to sit and drink. Though he often spoke of his South American roots,

Jorge had grown up in the area, had deep social ties in the neighborhood, and frequently told stories about playing on the beach in his youth. As we saw, when Randy enlisted him to sell his artwork in his absence, Jorge took to the job with a zeal I had not expected. He not only began working regular and consistent hours, but he took on increasing bouts of responsibility. He took some pride in reorganizing Randy's display, placing tables in an open-U shape so visitors could enter from the boardwalk and stand "inside" the designated space to peruse the artwork. But after a successful run of nearly a year, Jorge just suddenly stopped showing up.

Over six months later, as I walked on nearby Abbot Kinney Boulevard, Jorge popped his head out of the passenger window of a white van and waved energetically to me. He had a beaming smile; his hair was neatly cut and his face freshly shaven. Later that day, he came to me on the boardwalk where I was working. He told me he had decided to get sober and had left the job with Randy to get treatment. Now he was working in construction. He emphasized how happy he was to have a place to live, and recounted the recent joy he had felt when he received a bill and was able to pull open his nightstand drawer to grab the cash he needed to pay it.

Jorge said he was happy to see me and, looking at my own artwork, asked to purchase one of my watercolor paintings. When I told him I would give him one as a gift, he refused, insisting on paying the full ten dollars and informing me of his goal to collect artwork from everybody working in the marketplace. Another year later, Jorge was still working in construction, and came around now and again to say hello and catch up with some of his other friends.

In 2019, just over four years after I had last seen Jorge, I returned to the boardwalk and ran into him and his beaming smile by the recreation area. Jorge reported that he was still doing well; he stood tall as he told me that he had been sober for seven years. He was still living in the area and working in construction, making ends meet with his pay and the Social Security check he received. Jorge now positioned his work for Randy as a pathway toward sobriety and a construction job outside the boardwalk marketplace, something he wanted for himself.

In a society that sees "recovery" as a requirement for work, the local economy provided Jorge a rare opportunity to work *before* recovery. His story echoes some of those documented by the sociologist Teresa Gowan, who followed recyclers managing addiction as they contended with societal assumptions that "recovery" always precedes work. One of Gowan's participants, an admitted cocaine addict named Carlos, told her, "It's work which will get my head straight." But rather than use work as a way into recovery, his case workers required him to attend an Alcoholics Anonymous meeting every day. With such scheduling constraints, holding down a job became impossible. While I do not discredit the potential role of recovery in the lives of people like Carlos, we often ignore the needs of people who might want to participate in work activities *while recovering*—a process that will differ from person to person.

Jorge acknowledged the complications of being around addiction and his need to escape it. In 2019, he told me he couldn't really go "on the boardwalk" anymore—too many temptations and too many ways to get wrapped up. We were, at that moment, physically standing on the boardwalk, thus illustrating a meaningful distinction between the *physical* boardwalk and the *social* boardwalk. The statement also highlights the extreme pull of "the boardwalk" as more than a physical pathway: a magnetic social world capable of pulling people in and impacting their behavior. Again, the subversive safety net may support many people who believe there are few options, but it can also nab people who seek alternative ways of living.

The challenges of managing substance use are vast, and not everybody finds the services and support they need—be they within the subversive safety net or outside it—in time to save their life. When Anthony, an energetic man who often held signs to advertise a nearby pizza shop, was found dead about half a mile off the boardwalk, such consequences of this system came starkly into focus.

"They found his body on Lincoln," Tim told me, referencing the boulevard that forms the eastern boundary of the neighborhood. "Cirrhosis," he added.

The daily attempt to make precarity work does not always mean that it does—a possibility that nearly everybody in the boardwalk marketplace recognized. There were always clear limits to these practices, and the subversive safety net was not without its pitfalls. In fact, many of the experiences portrayed here should give us some pause and allow us to reflect critically on how and why people facing such dire circumstances find themselves here.

Conclusion

The boardwalk is an urban economy shaped profoundly by the life conditions of the people who produce it each day. As we have seen, these are people with extremely varied circumstances, though nearly all saw an incompatibility between their needs, conditions, and what was—or what they believed to be—available to them through formal institutions. Such incompatibility could be temporary: merely a gap in a credentialing process, an attempt to bypass arduous career development by being "discovered," or a bout of unemployment. Some workers might simply have held the view that wage work is inherently undignified, exploitative, and capitalistic. Others were unwilling or unable to get through the day without alcohol or drugs.

The daily activities and experiences discussed in this chapter are approached far more frequently through the lens of social problems, homelessness, or poverty than through the lens of work. People on the boardwalk developed an economic and social world within which different patterned relationships between drinking, drug use, and work emerged and became compatible. Those patterned relationships were interrelated, in that their complementarity was bound up with the very nature of work on the boardwalk.

Workers and law enforcement even co-policed the boundaries of appropriate substance use on the boardwalk to maintain that compatibility. For a subversive safety net to remain robust, it cannot be limitless—that is, not every substance-use practice is compatible with work, and on the boardwalk, workers ensured that people unable to commit to consistent economic activity, or whose reactions to substance use were highly disruptive to sales, were kept at bay. For police, the more that substance use became visibly tied to stigmatized identities and experiences (like homelessness or mental health problems), the more problematic it became. This form of precarious work was therefore not experienced in similar ways by all participants. Instead, the various constellations of life conditions worked to configure different forms of vulnerability. Such diversity of experience shaped power dynamics and social relations in ways that engendered both support *and* exploitation.

It is also important to remember that the people here were not untouched by social services and did not wholly disregard the potential for more conventional help—that is, their lives were hugely impacted by a smattering of interventions. Some received medical attention that included mental health diagnoses and access to prescription drugs. Others received assistance like TANF (Temporary Aid for Needy Families) and SSI (Supplemental Security Income). But the holes left in standard safety net programs are vast, and some people accessed and used such assistance in innovative and unintended ways.

In any case, I echo the concerns raised by other scholars of urban informality who caution that a focus on work activities might lead us to avert our eyes to suffering.[22] While this portrait allows us to see people's humanity, we should not refrain from a more critical interrogation of why people here managing serious dependency issues found that their preferred course of action was to tie themselves to the daily work, and the worker identities, of this urban marketplace. Furthermore, they often did so to carve out a place in which they could exist and community to which they could belong.

Up to this point, we have seen how people in the boardwalk economy made precarity work by producing a workplace, cultivating a community of workers, and incorporating many of the practices and behaviors often viewed as incompatible with work. Each wove another strand of the subversive safety net, producing a supportive social world that undermined many of the barriers people faced as they strove to meet their needs. This is the kind of invisible infrastructure that takes so much work to establish, and it is work we often ignore for a focus solely on the economic exchange.

At some point, however, people must make a buck, and making precarity work must involve making a sale. In the next chapter, I tease apart the varied considerations and moments of negotiation that go into making a sale. I show that the economic exchange is far more complicated than one might assume, as people here had to navigate the physical, legal, and social terrain of the boardwalk. I show how people collectively developed and shared such skills, allowing the boardwalk to be a generative space. This, then, weaves a final strand of the subversive safety net, giving it the generative potential that allows people to become public expressionists.

5

Making the Sale

I stood by Ricardo as he wove some leather around a small hoop with intense concentration. When he was satisfied, he pulled what appeared to be a string at the center, and, as if from nowhere, a beautiful web appeared inside the ring. He delicately attached a blue stone in the center and some feathers to dangle from the bottom before he hung it for display.

Ricardo was one of many vendors selling dream catchers, though he had been the first. Widely popularized in the 1960s and '70s as a symbol of Indigenous identity and culture, dream catchers were traditionally handmade using natural materials like willow reed. But the items have been appropriated for decades, detached from their cultural context, and hung on walls around the world with the rather simplified purpose to "catch bad dreams."

This is the "real material," Ricardo told me, making a clear distinction. "The others I sell are decorative," he said.

I asked Ricardo if he was annoyed that so many people had copied his idea and were now selling dream catchers as well. Counting multiple such vendors per block, it seemed to me they were everywhere.

"No," Ricardo said calmly. "They saw that it worked, and it caught fire."

But why Ricardo began selling dream catchers, how they "caught fire," and why he felt little resentment toward his competitors were all part of the process people in the boardwalk marketplace employed to decide what, when, where, and how to sell goods. In essence, this practice of making precarity work is about making the sale, and it is one that goes far beyond the economic exchange. I show in this chapter how decisions about what, when, where, and how to sell goods resulted from gaining the skills to navigate and adapt to the physical, legal, economic, and social terrain of the boardwalk. Producing and maintaining such generative potential wove an additional part of the subversive safety net, as it transforms the boardwalk from a venue for expression to a site of *becoming* an expressionist.

First, I show how people confronted the conditions of working in an unprotected outdoor environment and made decisions about the materials and mediums they used. I then consider the way people navigated the shifting regulation of permissible activities, modifying merchandise, changing the language used during an exchange, and blurring the boundaries of a "sale." Next, I show how participants performed a version of precarity they believed would be palatable to customers, balancing the "offbeat" grit visitors desired with both the mundanity of commercial resale and the harder-to-swallow harshness of poverty and inequality. Finally, I describe how participants developed and responded to perceptions of customer behavior, particularly as those behaviors were perceived to shift across time and space.

Throughout the chapter, I remain attuned to the way each one of these practices was embedded within a vibrant social world. People on the boardwalk existed within a web of relational entanglements. There were shared histories, friendships, and romances. There were moments of backstabbing and palpable grudges. There were idiosyncratic personalities, serious mental health issues, and intersecting forms of vulnerability. Intimate knowledge of this social terrain influenced decisions in complicated ways. Understanding how to make a sale is therefore highly consequential. It impacted when people worked and when they rested. It informed when it was time to save diligently or spend more freely.

Doing this correctly could mean the difference between profit and hefty fines, returning home or heading to jail.

A focus on social context offers greater insight into the way people make sense of economic action, and how these meaning-making processes explain what, when, and how people act in ways often left invisible by a rational economic actor approach.[1] In the end, a sociological analysis of making the sale takes us far beyond the momentary exchange of goods for money. In peeling back the layers of this process, we also learn how strategies to manage precarious conditions give a marketplace its dynamism. On the boardwalk, these strategies shaped product trends that spread like rashes and disappeared as quickly. They shaped ebbs and flows of competition over time and space. People here engaged in identity formation as this type of artist or that type of vendor. Their choices give meaning to other people's movement up and down the pathway, shaping fights over one space and avoidance over another. These strategies and decisions activated the boardwalk's infrastructure in new ways. Taken together, we see how this practice of making the sale created public access to adaptive skilling that afforded people durable opportunity in an ever-changing context. This weaves yet another strand of the subversive safety net, one that transforms the marketplace from a mere venue for public expression into a social world that generates public expressionists.

Navigating the Outdoors and Producing a Durable Object

Thud!

I jumped, easily startled as I was. The sound should have been familiar to me at that point, as I knowingly looked to Umar, who returned my glance with his idiosyncratic smirk. He walked to the middle of the pathway to pick up the framed seashells he had just tossed to the ground. His audience smiled—a potential customer he had hoped to entice with the durability of his craft. It was vivid proof for the traveler: no problem transporting these seemingly fragile shells. There was one thing participants quickly learned about selling merchandise on the boardwalk: the products had better be durable.

The very characteristics of the setting that drew many people to participate in the marketplace also became the challenges people faced as they worked. Southern California offered relief from a harsh winter, but the oceanfront pathway was no stranger to unforgiving sun, wind, fog, rain, sand, and dust. As workers set up their tables and stands along the western edge of the pathway, they also relinquished any physical protection from the passing crowds. There were wayward skateboards, physical fights, falling palm leaves, sprinklers, construction, and, of course, public surveillance. City regulation limited sunshade and canopies lest they block the ocean views. And all of this factored into what people made and sold.

"I've lost things to the wind," Chris told me. He recounted the moment a customer asked him the price of his painting, acrylic on canvas displayed on a large easel. "Four hundred," he had replied, only to watch as a gust of wind blew the painting to the ground, leaving a hole in the canvas. "Um, two hundred," he corrected.

It wasn't so bad on the boardwalk, he assured me, but moments like those could be rough when you depended on that income. As many of the artists here, Chris decided to turn his paintings into prints instead of originals. At first, he tried to display the prints in glass. But one day, a man was thrown into his artwork during a physical fight. Chris told me he had asked for some compensation, and the man gave it to him in the form of a loud "Fuck you!" There was rarely any recourse on the boardwalk, and at that point Chris made another quick decision—no glass.

In fact, turning to prints was such a common strategy that it sparked additional business on the boardwalk. Operating out of a small rental space down a tight corridor between beachfront buildings, a printer set up shop to meet the needs of vendors. With only a window to interact with customers, the printer took an original artwork, asked for desired measurements or edits, and returned a pile of prints for sale. In addition, the plastic envelopes this printer sold became a common way to display and sell prints.

There was no "welcome" pamphlet for new participants on the boardwalk. Word of mouth was a key to learning the tricks of the trade, and contrary to what we might assume about a competitive marketplace, people readily shared information to assist one another. "You know where to go, right?" Randy inquired when I had finished a few watercolor paintings. He then pointed me to the staircase that would lead me down a corridor and eventually to the hidden window. "They do all the prints for the vendors," he assured me.

There were also innovative workarounds for glass-free framing techniques. Sailor's small and colorful mixed-media designs were often finished with equally colorful "frames." The process, however, included gluing the artwork onto a larger wooden block and painting a border directly onto the wood. Both the paper and wood were then covered with a clear epoxy so the corners of the paper would not peel in the ocean air. The method was a success, and since participants witnessed its ability to resist moisture day after day, it was copied by others.

Beyond materials and mediums, the display method itself also had to resist the elements. Most vendors unpacked folding tables on which to display goods. They opted for colorful cloth, which they anchored down with clamps. If a vendor was displaying items flat, rocks often acted as paperweights. Most prints, however, were placed into bins for customers to comb through at their discretion. Hanging items were secured to racks and rods. And some vendors opted to place artwork directly on the ground.

I stood with Paul at his table when another vendor walked by wheeling merchandise. The cart got too close to Paul's table and knocked one of the legs out. In an instant, the table fell and merchandise went flying onto the floor. The man, who was profusely apologetic, joined Umar, Paul, and me to pick up the fallen goods. Umar gathered items energetically: small golden leaves, jewelry, tiny figurines. "Thanks," Paul said as I handed him some of the items I collected. Unfortunately, some of the figurines lost their tops, and a hand broke off of a small statue of Buddha. Paul threw the hand into the sand; there was little he could do. With a bit more optimism, Umar took one of the figurines and showed me how their broken parts would fit together. He had some glue at home, he told us, and would try to repair them.

Displays directly on the ground allowed some vendors to avoid the pitfalls of gravity. For instance, Jay displayed found objects from nature—or, at least, that was his claim. As a child, I owned a carved shell that was identical to the ones he displayed in a small bowl; my parents had purchased it at a souvenir store on a family vacation. He also sold driftwood he collected up and down the coast. And though I have no reason to believe he did not collect some of the driftwood, I could not ignore the tag I saw him clip from a bundle one day. But such details are neither here nor there on the boardwalk. The products themselves could withstand the elements because they were "of" the elements, and Jay marketed them as such: art directly from Mother Earth herself, he claimed. Placed on the ground atop a woven blanket, his merchandise was heavy enough to stay put in the wind, "natural" enough not to be harmed by dust and sand, and rather forgiving of any blemishes or breakages that might occur.

Still, there were always risks. "Can you move?" Jay said to Ivan, who was very intoxicated, standing quietly beside Jay and me and picking at some newly minted wounds. "You're getting blood on my stuff," he said as he nodded to the red circles forming on his blanket.

The conditions of working in a public outdoor marketplace were quickly felt by any individual who tried to make it work. The conditions will have their way. Wind will dictate the way you display goods. The salt air will challenge adhesives. The sun will fade colors. Fights, skateboards, dogs, and children will add unpredictable threats to goods and merchandise. In the end, there is no recourse for such realities; rather, people must learn to navigate the conditions of a marketplace by constructing durable goods. These processes materially manifested in the type of objects for sale along the boardwalk and the type of artist or vendor one became.

Hazel painted colorful contemporary images on canvas and displayed her work on easels. With a price far below that of Chris's, she was less concerned with damage than he had been. She wore overalls splattered in paint and lived in a community well known for its art, about twenty miles away. But Hazel did not come to Venice to make art. Her arrival was a familiar story: a break with family, a rupture in her life, a bout with drugs, and the recognition that she needed a change. That is, she did not come to the boardwalk as an artist in need of a marketplace. She found the marketplace and slowly *became* an artist. And because of this trajectory, the conditions of the boardwalk largely shaped the type of artist she became. "You can't do oils out here," she said to me. Early in my attempts to set up and try my hand at painting, I naively assumed the medium would be up to me. But beyond my lack of talent, I also noticed that sitting and waiting for oil to dry was a difficult time investment and untenable approach to producing and selling artwork on the boardwalk. Hazel caught me early and admitted to having made a similar mistake in her early days. "Too much dust and sand," she confirmed. This was the very reason why she learned to paint with acrylic: it has a fast drying time.

The fast drying time was not just about producing work at a faster pace. It also had to do with the fact that much of a painter's painting time was spent on the boardwalk itself. The reason was threefold. First, the time commitment necessary to establish oneself in the marketplace left little time "off" the boardwalk to work. Second, customers often wanted to witness the artist working, hoping to catch a glimpse behind the curtain. And third, the restrictions around commercial resale encouraged many participants to "create" their products in real time, even if these creations were thinly veiled marketing for other products being sold. As a result, the medium had to be beachfront friendly.

Producing a Permissible Sale

Throughout this book, I have discussed the role of shifting regulation. The city not only regulated forms of access, as I covered in chapter 2, but also the products being sold. Los Angeles Municipal Code 42.15 changed more than once during my time on the boardwalk. Each version set forth new standards for participation in the marketplace and sparked both successful and unsuccessful challenges to those standards.

There were two key standards for regulating goods over the course of my research and they were largely known to people by their respective nicknames: "inextricably intertwined" and "nominal utility." With both versions, people could not "hawk, peddle, vend or sell, or request or solicit donations for, any goods, wares, merchandise, foodstuff or refreshments" on the boardwalk. In other words, in accordance with the rest of Los Angeles, the ordinance prohibited public vending.

What made the boardwalk unique, however, were the *exceptions* to this restriction. First, the "inextricably intertwined" standard stated the following exceptions:

- "newspapers, magazines, periodicals, or other printed matter commonly sold or disposed of by news vendors"
- "[the] sale of merchandise constituting, carrying or making a religious, political, philosophical or ideological message or statement which is inextricably intertwined with the merchandise"
- "sales or soliciting of donations [by] any performer or musician engaging in constitutionally protected activities . . . any painter, sculptor or photographer, provided the painter, sculptor or photographer is displaying his or her own original creations and/or limited editions"

This version of the ordinance therefore received its nickname from one of its most vulnerable phrases: "inextricably intertwined." The phrase had a life of its own; it was debated and misstated, and often cropped up in conversation as "intrinsically intertwined." Its slippery meaning was lamented, celebrated, challenged, and embraced. But debates aside, it was once the key to making precarity work on the boardwalk.

One day, RJ and I sat with Tim behind the table that he had set up for the day. Per usual, Tim had displayed a variety of items, including some incense he had purchased and some he had made himself. RJ's jewelry was displayed on a portion of the table as well: cheaply made mass-produced necklaces purchased from a retail store in downtown LA. As we sat, a man walked up to the

table. He was tall and slim, likely in his late thirties or early forties. He wore an LA City Recreation and Parks badge—during the
months of my research when that meant something—around his
neck and an ID that read "Alston." His slow-moving body language suggested something between resignation and reluctance,
which he further communicated when he told Tim with a rather
unenthused lack of inflection that he was just out "busting balls"
for the day. He began explaining to Tim that he could not sell the
goods he had on display. He spoke low, saying something vague
about "the ordinance" and "self-expression." "This isn't what
they had in mind . . ." Alston said more clearly as he surveyed
Tim's products. "They need to be something you've created," he
said. Tim responded excitedly. The incense is "homemade!" he
said. But Alston pushed further. "Well, I wouldn't say you've cre-
aaa-ted the incense," he said, holding onto the word *created* in
a way that seemed to admit the subjectivity of it all. "It's about
freedom of expression" he reiterated. "A message of expression
has to be intertwined." He gave Tim an example: "Like you can
sell a T-shirt if it says STOP THE WAR. But there has to be an apparent purpose or message."

The ordinance may have provided the official statement on
allowable activities on the boardwalk, but without a formal registration process, there was no assurance that people had ever received, read, or agreed to such guidelines. So, it was often through
interactions like this that the regulation hit the ground. Alston
communicated intentions, blurry boundaries, areas of vulnerability, and examples. He talked about what city officials "had in
mind." And when he told Tim, "I wouldn't say you've *created* the
incense," he not only highlighted areas where the boundaries of
permissibility were fuzzy but also indicated how Tim might run
into problems. Finally, he offered a concrete example of a T-shirt
proclaiming STOP THE WAR. The Free Speech Zone, he implied,
should appropriately be used as a space for political and ideological messaging.

Exactly what constitutes political and ideological messaging
is debatable. On the boardwalk, such messaging was often subjective. Furthermore, it was tethered to a romanticized image

of the beatniks and hippies of the 1950s and '60s. It was this bohemian history that still resonated with many Venetians and visitors alike: one that was largely white, conveniently divorced from the American civil rights movement, detached from contemporary experiences of poverty, and retroactively justified in its disillusionment with the establishment.[2] Even when Alston told Tim he could sell a STOP THE WAR T-shirt, he more readily conjured an image of the anti-Vietnam War movement of the 1960s than he did opposition to the then-current war in Afghanistan. In the end, participants were often required to understand *which* version of political and ideological messaging was permissible.

Tim may have struggled, or at least feigned confusion, but Ousmane got the message loud and clear. Ousmane was a Senegalese immigrant who lamented the satisfaction many people felt with long-term work on the boardwalk. "This is not paradise," he would assure me as he gestured to the expanse of soft sand and sparkling blue ocean in the distance. Ousmane was well educated; the depth of his knowledge about everything from global politics to literature was intimidating. He spoke multiple languages. He read Tolstoy while he waited for customers. He was a trained interpreter and claimed to have worked with the United Nations. On the boardwalk, however, he sold hats, bags, and T-shirts adorned with the colors green, yellow, red, and black. Ousmane was one of the many Black men, mostly of West African origin, nicknamed the "Rasta guys" for their merchandise—goods purchased from downtown Los Angeles and resold on the boardwalk. He was aware the goods were mass-produced, but Ousmane still believed the Rasta colors satisfied the "inextricably intertwined" standard. Green for the land. Yellow for the wealth. Red for the blood. "These are expressions of African identity," Ousmane told me. But he had been explicitly informed by law enforcement that such items did not reflect the *type* of expressive message intended by the ordinance. And since Ousmane did not care all that much, he altered the items.

Ousmane walked me over to a hat. He picked it up and flipped it upside down, revealing a small white tag with the word LOVE printed in black. He looked at me and shrugged. "If the city wants it to have a message, I'll sew in a message," he said rather unenthusiastically. He walked over to a few other items and flipped them over. A belt had a tag stating PEACE. A bag had a tag with the image of a peace sign. If he sewed these in, he told me, officials couldn't say it was "just commercial." Rather than try to defend the expression of pan-African identity, Ousmane opted for the "peace and love" message so iconically tied to the flower children and hippies of the 1960s.

For the most part, Ousmane was able to continue working on the boardwalk until he received formal employment and promptly left Los Angeles for New York City. Yet, defining what was and was not "inextricably intertwined" remained a challenge. And when vendors began receiving more fines for commercial items, many decided to avoid issues by forgoing defense of their products and playing on the very definition of vending itself—that is, they exploited another vulnerable phrase in the ordinance: "Nor shall the provisions of this section prohibiting sales or soliciting of donations apply to any performer or musician engaging in constitutionally protected activities."

"It's all by donation," Jay would say. "People usually give me a donation of five [dollars] for that," Tim offered. Few customers noticed the subtle phrasing, but for vendors, a slip could be highly consequential. When RJ told me he was not making "much right now," he added some of his added challenges. The profit he made from vending was his "bread and butter," he told me. Then he clarified: "[It] subsidizes my GR, and it's just enough," he said, referring to the General Relief funds he received. The EBT (Electronic Benefits Transfer, formerly food stamps) was for the food, he told me—about $220. "But money is the hard part to keep," RJ said, meaning cash. And keeping it was made even harder by unforeseen fines. "I went to court for giving a price on the boardwalk, and I had to pay to do the community service. I did that." Many participants learned (and were reminded) of similar lessons; *how* one sold merchandise could be as important as *what* one sold. And so, vendors played on the meaning of "a sale" by blurring the lines of the transaction.

Marcus told me that the cops tried to ticket him, but he insisted he was not selling anything. He knowingly exploited the "donation" clause that allowed a monetary exchange for constitutionally protected activities. "See," he told me, "I'm selling pamphlets and giving the oils away for free." He continued, "So the cops come up and say, 'You can't sell that!' and I say, 'I'm not selling anything. I can *display* anything here. I'm getting money for the pamphlets, and that's free speech.'" He confirmed that of course he knew the legal issues well. He may not have more than a high school education, he told me, but he knew the issues well. While we spoke, Marcus had a few customers. I watched as he offered samples of his merchandise. When one man selected four bottles of oil and held out the money to pay, Marcus said, "Here is your pamphlet. The other stuff is for free." He pulled out a pamphlet and flipped it over to show me a bar code on the back connected to his website. He turned to me to reiterate: "I'm really selling the pamphlet, not the oils."

In 2010, however, the same lawsuit that ended the Public Expression Participant Permit Program discussed in chapter 2 also invalidated the "inextricably intertwined" standard. Ruled "void for vagueness" by the Ninth Circuit, the 2011 amendment returned to prior language that permitted only goods with no more than "nominal utility." In the time between the Ninth Circuit ruling and the new ordinance, I attended numerous neighborhood council subcommittee meetings. Optimistic residents and participants debated methods to allow for handmade knitwear and jewelry, since both were deemed to have some greater utility than a painting might. Understanding the city's goal to be the restriction of commercial goods, they floated ideas like the credentialing and registration of artisans. But in the end, the city opted for the precedence of the "nominal utility" standard and banned "housewares, appliances, clothing, sunglasses, auto parts, oils, incense, perfume, crystals, lotions, candles, jewelry, toys and stuffed animals."

Such clarity, however, provided both new constraints and opportunities. If we have learned one thing, it is that people do not give up so easily. The implementation of the "nominal utility" standard was most visible through the relative disappearance of clothing and jewelry. And since commercial goods often proliferated within various immigrant networks, the "nominal utility" standard had the biggest impact on the West African men selling Rasta-wear clothing and Latin American vendors selling colorful bracelets, rings, and necklaces. Many people who had been selling goods purchased by an "employer"—typically an established member of the co-ethnic community with the capital to buy commercial products in large quantities, distribute them to other co-ethnics, and take a commission—left the marketplace when the ticketing began. The regulation of goods therefore had a racialized impact, one that even Tim had warned of prior to the "nominal utility" standard. As he told me once, if you get rid of "intrinsically intertwined," it would just be "the Hazels and the Jays" out here, referencing two participants who held in common their whiteness and general adherence to the peace and love of American hippiedom.

The regulation also sparked new ways of selling goods and further blurred boundaries between the formal east-side economy and the informal west-side economy. In fact, the "nominal utility" standard had *spatial* consequences, reorganizing people and practices, shuffling vendors and merchandise around the pathway, and activating once-dormant nooks and crannies. Rasta wear and jewelry suddenly appeared on the inland side of the boardwalk, hung in unused doorways and open walls. Merchants who had long been publicly opposed to commercial vending on public space suddenly seemed quite eager to capitalize on their infrastructure and rent such space to those very same vendors.

William was one of the vendors who migrated east. Using a stretch of bare wall between two stores, William mounted a mesh screen that served as a display area to hang his handmade jewelry—delicate gold earrings and pendants made from real leaves. He also placed a small table and chair against the wall, allowing for a small but functional setup. He even posted a sign stating that he accepted credit cards.

"So, you were able to move over here, huh?" I asked one day.

"Yeah," William said, adding that he had tried to stay on the west side, but the cops "got him." He had hoped to navigate the ban on jewelry by laying his pendants flat so they did not appear to be jewelry. But as luck would have it, one police officer had also been a former customer. The cop had purchased a necklace for his wife months earlier, so he held up the gold leaf next to a gold chain to prove as much. William now paid rent for an outdoor wall on the east side of the pathway. "I have a view of the beach now," he told me, contented. "But the sun is brutal."

William was frustrated by the blurred boundaries, stating that he and others were artisans and craftspeople, but the issue was that the city lacked the resources to designate them as such. He believed that in Santa Monica he would get a permit because they would have some kind of a coordinator to prove he was an artist and permit him to sell. But Venice was different. "It's just this public expression zone; it's vague" he said. He then posed the question: Are artisans and craftspeople public expression[ists]? Unquestionably they are, he answered. But the problem was that it "opens up the doors."

Michelle, on the other hand, did not try to prove she was an artisan to anybody. She sold mass-produced clothing and jewelry and simply needed to find a space to do so. She moved south, past designated spot 1, and onto a part of the pathway squeezed between small kiosks and a recreation area. She rented a wooden cabinet that jutted out of the wall, not so dissimilar to a bathroom vanity cabinet. But it afforded some perks. She could lock it with a padlock overnight to store her goods. And when opened, the double doors served as a display rack for clothing. Each day, she put a table and chair in front of the cabinet, setting up shop in the minimal amount of space afforded by one of the most narrow and crowded sections of the boardwalk. Relatively speaking, she found the arrangement acceptable, and though she told me she missed "the family," hers proved a long-term solution: when I met up with Michelle years later during a visit from the East Coast, she was in the same spot. She smiled and gave me a hug, proud to confirm that the now-nearly-six-foot man leaning against the wall next to her was indeed her son, all grown up. He had been one of the many small children who ran around the boardwalk during my research, supported by the community of workers we met in chapter 3. Michelle had kept up the business and her ability to support her family.

To participate in the boardwalk marketplace, people needed to adjust and adapt.[3] They altered the goods. They shifted the way they sold those goods. And they found new locations from which to sell. In the process, they blurred the boundaries between the "public" Free Speech Zone and the "private" rental spaces, further blurring the lines between so-called formal and informal economies. Such decision-making led to movement across time and space—sparking the very dynamism that is often taken for granted and left unexamined.

Performing Precarity

Participants in the boardwalk marketplace were keenly aware that it was more than their products for sale—they themselves were part of the attraction. As with many other tourist destinations and marketplaces, people consumed much more than merchandise. They were buying an experience, a memory. They desired some symbol of the place they were temporarily inhabiting. The public identity of Venice as a site of counterculture and its history as a bohemian enclave were key to this experience.[4] But what it means to *be* bohemian today is less clear. The precarious life conditions of so-called bohemians, the Beats and hippies of the 1950s and '60s, were often seen as a choice, a resistance from "below." The precarious life conditions of those who have been pushed to the social and economic margins were often seen as the ugly result of advanced capitalism and neoliberal policy and ideology, a degradation from "above." But many people here who found themselves marginalized by social, legal, and economic systems adopted the language of bohemia to explain their social position and daily conditions. Their choices may have also toed a line between so-called resistance and so-called degradation.

Visitors to the boardwalk were rarely interested in teasing these distinctions apart. In fact, many customers consumed the very symbols of precarious life conditions: Rennie's BUM SIGNS were no more than cardboard-and-crayon pleas for help. Randy's broken skateboards served as an artist's canvas, but they were also refuse collected from the nearby skate park. JP's garbage sculpture was quite literally rummaged trash glued together, the creative effort of a man living on the street. Even those with means for new items, clean tablecloths, and newly laundered clothes knew they must strike a balance between the unconventional and the dispossessed. Paul made sure to cover his table in a paint-splattered sheet. Jay used a woven blanket to display his goods directly on the ground. Those working on the boardwalk were selling a story as much as an object.

As I mentioned earlier, many artists chose to create their work directly on the boardwalk, a way of proving their art was an original creation while also allowing visitors to experience the production process. Many visitors expected more than a display of finished work, making Venice less of a gallery and more like a studio. The value of Hazel's fast-drying acrylic not only avoided the problem of dust and sand, but it also fit well with these performative demands of the boardwalk. But such public displays meant that "private" moments were difficult. When I sat one day painting, I suddenly felt a person standing directly behind my chair, head tilted, watching me draw. Tourists often behaved in ways indicative of their right to be in close proximity. And since workers knew that visitors wanted to consume our behavior, many of us complied. This meant that the best materials were not only durable as a finished product but could also withstand the production process in an outdoor environment. When Umar threw his artwork onto the ground, he too added to this performative character of the marketplace—showing, rather than telling, his customers that they could throw those seashells in their luggage with confidence.

The performative aspect of the boardwalk could also extend beyond the boardwalk. I watched as a few teenage boys approached Randy with a Flip Video camera in hand. They asked Randy to freestyle—a request that somewhat bewildered me, since Randy's display included spray-painted artwork. But as Randy considered the offer, he asked the boy holding the camera if he planned to give him a tip for the performance. The boys looked at one another, a little confused, then finally agreed. And so, Randy complied and began freestyle rapping for the camera.

Unfortunately for the eager audience, the Flip lost its charge and died mid-performance. Immediately, another boy pulled out his iPhone, aimed it at Randy, and recorded the rest of the rap.

Randy had delivered everything the boys had hoped for. Excitedly, they put their hands in the air to meet Randy's. "That was awesome!" one of them confirmed. Randy was not ready to give up on the exchange, however, and told the boys to do him a favor. "Post it on MySpace or Facebook," he said, "and put a link to my website." Then the boys went to give a tip, but rather than confidently place some money in the bucket, they looked at one another for a bit. Randy must have interpreted the confusion and reluctance in their body language because he quickly told them, "Change is fine." They eventually dropped what looked to be pennies and nickels in the bucket.

Randy turned to me to clarify—or possibly justify—what had taken place. "I do a bunch of those every day," he said, though it had been the first I witnessed. Then he told me he figured he'd be "all over the place" in no time. While I never witnessed the fruits of Randy's endeavors, he was not alone in his hope to have his talent discovered. Compact discs could be sampled, websites visited, and QR codes scanned.

And yet, there were limits. Rather than an artist simply giving the customers what they wanted, the awareness of being consumed also informed acts of resistance. One day, Hazel came up to me to inform me that Khaled was a talented artist. I knew of his ability, since he had been teaching me some watercolor techniques. However, I did not know the extent of it. I approached Khaled about his artwork and asked why he would not choose to sell it, knowing that original artwork was the surest way to avoid fines for misusing the marketplace. It turned out that Khaled did not want to put his own work on display. It was too personal, he said, and he didn't want customers rifling through his creations, haggling to save a buck for their own enjoyment. Instead, he would stick to purchasing mass-produced merchandise, and should the customer assume it was made with his own hands, he would not contradict them. The act of denying tourists access to his own artwork was Khaled's way of asserting control and autonomy. It allowed him the privacy of his own creativity.

There was also limited support for "success," as became clear when one of the boardwalk's larger marijuana dispensaries was taken over by a then-unknown social media platform called Snapchat. As we learned in chapter 1, Snapchat began modestly when recent Stanford grads opened up shop, but it soon developed into Snap Inc., with one of the largest IPOs in Los Angeles history.[5] In fact, Snap Inc. joined the booming tech industry building itself up around the boardwalk, which also included Google's LA headquarters. The neighborhood hosted events with merchandise sporting its new moniker: Silicon Beach. But as we also learned in chapter 1, Snap Inc. began purchasing property near the boardwalk and became the target of disdain from those who believed the more "commercial" side of the economy was antithetical to the boardwalk's culture. There was an ongoing tension between the dream of "making it" within precarious conditions and the disdain for what becomes of someone who has "made it." As I have said previously, making precarity work in places like the boardwalk must always be *in the making*.

Deciding When and Where to Sell

"Yesterday was awful," Umar told me.

I was surprised by this, since it had been so crowded. I told him as much.

"There were tons of people," he clarified, "but nobody buying anything." For Umar, this was a huge disappointment. He lamented getting up at 4 a.m. and getting home at 8 p.m. All for nothing. "A hundred maybe," he said, "it's not worth it." His face exuded frustration and exhaustion—a far cry from his characteristic cheeriness.

Without any guarantee of income, people working on the boardwalk were forced to make tough decisions about the value of a day's work. For people like Umar, who drive long distances and support families, it was necessary to weigh the cost of gas and loss of time with the promise of profit. But all of this was relative, requiring an intricate understanding of profits in relation to time and space. Participants used these relative metrics to develop their understanding of "good days" and "bad days," of profitable blocks and those deemed worthless. They relied on subtle indicators of customer behavior; it wasn't just seeing people that mattered, but knowing when their wallets would open. They watched the customer's body language and habits. They navigated the fuzzy boundaries between attractions and distractions. They tried to balance gathering information from other participants with retaining some semblance of secrecy and competitive edge. This informed people when to work hard, when to nap, when to save, and when to spend.

I walked with Tim to his spot. "Ricardo made three hundred yesterday," he said.

"But he came late yesterday," I replied instinctually, "not until about noon or so."

Seemingly aware of this, Tim drew some conclusions. "I really need somebody to make some feather earrings for me; that's what is selling like crazy!"

Tim had been watching, and increasingly, women visiting the boardwalk were purchasing earrings with long dangling feathers—a kind of bohemian aesthetic that fit well with Venice's beach vibe. Convinced he was not capable of such crafts, he offered to pay me to make them for him, and his enthusiasm bulldozed right over my refusal. "They need to be long feathers with a hair clip at the end—that's what everybody is buying!"

As Tim illustrates, the public setting allowed participants a way to gauge successes and failures. Merchandise was not hidden in private space; purchases were rarely concealed in bags or boxes. Participants had front-row seats to one another's business, as merchandise sat there untouched or as a vendor's stock dwindled by sunset. They saw fines distributed, heard rumors of police encounters, or watched as LAPD sedans rolled by. Even when participants remained stuck in place throughout the day (as they often were), consumers inadvertently sent waves of communication up and down the boardwalk by promenading their purchases: artwork tucked under their arms, new jewelry on their wrists, necks, and earlobes, henna tattoos displayed on their skin. Successes and failures were shared between otherwise distant participants, and it didn't take long for people to gain a sense of what sold and what didn't.

I could see Khaled walking energetically back to the table. I had been helping him sell vintage tins for a few weeks and it wasn't uncommon for us to leave one another for a bit. The tins were his most recent strategy to bypass new restrictions. And since customers seemed satisfied with his claims of having personally printed the tins with such images, he was still gathering information on his profit margins. "They're all complaining how slow it is today," Khaled said excitedly. "Ten dollars. Thirty dollars." He rattled off the numbers he was hearing from others. "A hundred dollars is great," he concluded about his own profits. "And for a Thursday by two p.m." This was a "good day," Khaled confirmed.

But "good" and "bad" days were never just about dollars and cents. As both Umar and Khaled mentioned, it was about measuring profits alongside other shifting metrics. How were the crowds? What day of the week was it? What time of year? What time of day? When Michelle told me about making only twenty dollars one day, she concluded it was "not that bad." She said this specifically because she hadn't arrived until about 2 p.m., and she knew the time of year itself was slow. "It will pick up with the holidays, and then it will be slow again until spring break," she assured me. So, the twenty bucks was at least "something," she said.

Like with many economies that rely on seasonal demand, boardwalk participants were keenly aware of the ebbs and flows of tourists and profit. While summer months proved the most profitable, the winter holidays and spring break brought important flows of cash during the year that could stretch until the crowds returned in June. When Khaled made five hundred dollars one weekend during spring break, he told me definitively that the money he makes in March had better last through June. "That's the way it works," he said.

Such knowledge informed significant and consequential life decisions. When Khaled knew he had extra money in hand, he often stayed at a motel rather than in his van. When things were slow, he picked up some construction work on the boardwalk; in this rapidly gentrifying neighborhood, there was plenty. Paul ran errands in the morning, when people were unlikely to be purchasing artwork. Tim used slow days to drive downtown and purchase more merchandise. Emma chose the days to complete her community service. Ricardo and Randy often traveled to other festivals around the country, taking advantage of more secure pockets of profit where possible.

And while time was an important metric for success on the boardwalk, it was not the only metric. Participants also considered the relative value of space when choosing where to set up their goods. And not all areas of the pathway were considered equal. Parking lots were believed to concentrate crowds by providing initial starting and ending points for one's visit. Food kiosks and restaurants were believed not only to attract people, but to encourage them to "open their wallets." As participants developed perceptions of customer behavior across space, they constructed mental maps of hidden treasures and notable pitfalls. These maps informed key decisions about where to set up and what to expect from customers once there.

The Venice boardwalk was often a vibrant scene replete with a dizzying array of sights, scents, and sounds. To the north, however, the pathway abruptly transformed into the serenity of Santa Monica. This was a visceral boundary more than a physical one, and Rose Avenue commonly marked this transition from the buzz of the commercial corridor to the calm of senior citizen housing. The pathway then widened into a park and the buildings receded. The music faded and the sound of ocean waves suddenly became audible. To use Southern California lingo: it was a very different vibe.

Yet, there was still a cluster of "designated spaces" north of Rose. "No-man's-land," as a vendor told me. It was a nickname that arose from perceptions of how visitors moved through space, and how these movements created zones of transition that led to low profits. Specifically, the understanding was that people walking south from Santa Monica would not yet be prepared for Venice. They were likely out for a beachfront stroll, unprepared for the boardwalk marketplace. Even if they did see some merchandise they liked, folks believed it might take them some time to acclimate and spend money. Conversely, visitors walking north would likely feel the energy plummet when they crossed Rose. Having perceived their destination as Venice rather than Santa Monica, they were likely to turn around and head back the way they came. Such perceptions of movement were rarely about explaining people's enjoyment of the space and more often about explaining differences in profit. Recall that it was a space in this no-man's-land that had caused a vendor some remorse when a newcomer offered to "buy" it for a hundred dollars. The vendor had offloaded it for the entire weekend, feeling guilty that the cost outweighed the likely profit.

"It's about a hundred dollars for every block you go south until you hit Horizon," Niall told me, marking the southern boundary as an outdoor café at Horizon Avenue. And while there is reason to believe that this was not a perfect calculation, its veracity is not the most important factor. Niall was revealing a mental map of the boardwalk that many vendors shared. And this map created very real competition over certain spaces, concentrating them in the hands of longtime participants and making them more difficult to access.

As a result, there were a cluster of seemingly ideal spaces that became home to more arguments over one's "right" to space. Here, there were more visible moments of aggression and intimidation when newcomers attempted to set up. These spaces required earlier arrival times and informal agreements. Furthermore, because such desirability left these spaces in the hands of longtime participants, their personal histories and social entanglements ran deep. Those entanglements became highly consequential when they erupted in arguments, blossomed into relationships, withered into breakups, and sparked temporary and long-term relocations.

Put another way, on the mental map of the boardwalk, this region would be named Drama. And drama can complicate the value of even the most profitable spaces.

Kristen sold small paintings just south of Rose Avenue. Here, a cluster of painters, sculptors, and artisans often set up their goods. For Kristen, the same calculation of profit margins that created more competition to the south became the very reason that she opted to stay north. It was calm here, she told me. And people got along. Kristen told me she had built community up here, and these were not the vendors opting for the biggest profit margins, nor were they the kind of people who wanted to argue over spaces. As a result, the area tended to avoid more commercial goods and lean more heavily toward original artwork. "[Up here,] it's more about art," Kristen said. She pointed south. Down there, it was "the two-dollar stuff" and there was "too much drama."

People's personalities and behavior greatly impacted the decisions of others. And people could shift the relative value of a "good" space and throw others' cost-benefit analysis into a tailspin. Chris told me that Mo was a huge problem because he tried to "own" those spaces, he said as he motioned to a group of spaces in front of a popular café. "That would have to be the *last* space on the boardwalk for me to take it. I'd rather be right up by Santa Monica than next to him," Chris said, confirming just how low a spot next to Mo was on his list. Chris explained that Mo would put amplified drums right behind him until Chris left. "As if the drums weren't loud enough, they have them amplified," he said. For these reasons, Chris would rather be in no-man's-land. Hidden beneath decisions of where to set up one's goods were such complicated understandings of the boardwalk's *social* world.

But participants needed not only to consider their own position within that social world. They also had to consider the way visitors might experience it. Were visitors comfortable, annoyed, or distracted? Were they likely to view goods as "art" or as "crap?" In other words, whether one was selling "art" or "crap" could be a matter of context. After all, one's goods sat next to those of their neighbors. They heard one another's conversations, were impacted by their visitors, abutted their display of merchandise, smelled their weed, heard their music, vied for the same customers, and shared in their public surveillance.

JP was a white man in his fifties who lived on the street. He decided to make sculptural artwork from found materials— discarded items lying around the neighborhood, and some found in the garbage. JP arrived one day by bike, pulling a wooden wagon with wheels, and saw the spot that RJ had vacated for the day and told JP to use. As JP unhitched his wagon and set it up in the spot, he looked over at Jeff's neatly arranged display. "I've got to be next to him?! I might as well be in an alley in the worst part of town. It's like an alley-gutter Venice dude next to a Beverly Hills extravaganza." He did not move, but he made things clear: "I am not happy about this situation."

Perceiving how customers experienced one's goods in relation to others added another layer of consideration. "I like Randy, but he's yelling all day, so it's hard if you're next to him," Jay told me. Randy was a hawker. He yelled out short catchphrases to the passing public, eager to get people's attention and draw them to his artwork. He was loud and often called to specific people as they walked by. The vast majority were women, whom he made aware of his attention by referencing their appearance, be it attire, hairstyle, or other physical attributes. "He kills sales if you're next to him" Jay continued, complaining that the yelling simply "wore people out," the result of which was that they wanted to get away. It wasn't personal for Jay: "I respect him, though; he's working hard and does well because he sells for cheap."

But even Randy could be out-hawked and had to balance his own desire to be heard with those of others. When Randy moved from one of the most coveted blocks to a space across from the Venice Freakshow, he had to contend with the ongoing amplified announcements. "Step right up, folks!" The MC yelled. "We've got the five-legged dog. The Bearded Lady. The Tattooed Man." It was hard to hear Randy in that context, and during the weekend shows, visitors often directed their attention to the charismatic MC. But Randy liked the crowds, he told me. And, as he reiterated multiple times, he appreciated that there was less drama on this end.

Accepting the Public Affair

For years, Randy painted stenciled signs on the surface of broken skateboards. I stood with him when a couple of guys came by one day asking why he didn't have any. "I don't do them anymore," he said. When I asked him to explain, he told me that "somebody" copied him. That somebody had been Jaden, who worked nearby and was a long-standing participant. Rather than continue creating similar items, Randy's response had been to "let him have it."

Jaden hadn't copied Randy for fun. He had been working as a successful artisan on the boardwalk for years, making handcrafted instruments. But instruments have more than "nominal utility," and when that standard was reintroduced into the ordinance in 2011, Jaden took up painting. And with the skate park just off the boardwalk, broken boards were an easy and appealing surface to come by. In fact, Mitchell, a longtime resident and frequent visitor to the boardwalk, began picking them up and distributing them to vendors for a small fee. So, not long after taking up painting, Jaden was painting on skateboards as well.

While we might expect competition to drive fierce arguments over one's right to artwork and merchandise, the boardwalk often operated on a "live and let live" policy. The public nature of the boardwalk marketplace shaped power dynamics and lessened community sanctions in ways that differed from the strict rules against competition we might find elsewhere. In fact, Randy once published a manual with explicit directions on "how to make it." The guide offered suggestions of specific items that sell well on the boardwalk. Unfortunately, Randy's guide highlighted specific products rather than the kinds of constraints participants would need to consider, so in the face of shifting regulations and changing trends, many of his suggestions were no longer valid. Still, his behavior is indicative of the ways that workers communicated with one another, shared ideas, and generally supported the ideology of making precarity work, even if that meant tapping into one another's ideas.

Over the course of research, I saw several copied crafts: incense recipes, stencil paintings, wood carvings, and spray-painted art, to name a few. However, I never saw an argument erupt over this, nor did I hear this discussed as a major overstep. Occasionally people would talk about being the "original," and only once did I talk with a vendor who said he had initiated a price-cutting strategy to eliminate a copycat. Unsurprisingly, the strategy failed. Instead, it was far more common for workers to accept that copying would and did take place as the mere result of a community making precarity work.

Conclusion

Returning to this chapter's opening scene, Ricardo's decision to sell dream catchers had little to do with a personal expression of identity or an artistic affinity for the craft. It was a pragmatic decision, evidence of how he navigated the physical, social, economic, and legal terrain of the boardwalk. When the ordinance banned jewelry, he had been stuck with an existing supply of leather that he had once used for bracelets. He had the tools and skills to fasten jewelry together, along with the adornments of beads and those feather earrings that had once been so popular. Not only could these materials be repurposed, but at least some of the dream catchers could be publicly handmade, as Ricardo sat on a stool crafting the items. And—at least, according to the city officials tasked with enforcing the ordinance—the utility of dream catching was convincingly "nominal." It was a plus, of course, that the items were virtually unbreakable, and once adhered to a wooden rod over his table, the wind worked to enhance the beauty of the item rather than obscure it.

The final layer of Ricardo's decision came from recognizing and exploiting the subjectivity of expression. As it turned out, Ricardo's Mexican identity was difficult to disentangle from an Indigenous identity and could go unquestioned by the largely white police force regulating the boardwalk. As one of many different phases of Ricardo's work on the boardwalk, this was his new success. And initially, as I mentioned at the start of this chapter, he was the only dream-catcher vendor on the western edge.

When dream catchers "caught fire" and other vendors, almost all of whom were Latino, also began selling them up and down the pathway, Ricardo had shrugged, seemingly unfazed by the competition. He understood that his success would be publicly visible and, as a result, up for grabs. He was aware how the knowledge of customers' purchases would travel up and down the pathway. The newest regulation had caused an upheaval, and many people were searching for something new. "They saw that it worked," he said, "and it caught fire."

Making a sale goes far beyond explaining what, when, where, and how people sold goods on the boardwalk. It helps explain the dynamism of the boardwalk—a dynamism that also characterizes the subversive safety net. While many of the people working here remained for years, and even decades, there was always change. Products appeared and faded; people shifted locations. The boardwalk's marketplace was far from static. But the opportunity to develop and publicly witness how new products succeed or fail afforded people more durable opportunities to work in a context that was constantly changing. People did not fear legal recourse for infringing on intellectual property rights.[6] There was no pattern of violent sanctions. It was one more indication that this social world emerged as more than the sum of its parts. People were not atomistically pursuing their own interests; they had to invest in the kind of social system that allowed all to adjust and adapt.

This, then, wove another strand of the subversive safety net: building a social world to which people could arrive on the boardwalk and learn to *become* a public expressionist. The marketplace was not a mere venue, though it might be seen that way on the surface. Instead, it was a dynamic social system with generative potential.

A Subversive Safety Net

Throughout this book, I have shown how people live and labor on the edge. Using the case of the Venice boardwalk, I have documented the way people made precarity work. They organized socially and strategically to navigate, and undermine, the regulation of public space. They negotiated, mitigated, and exploited one another's precarious circumstances to reach their goals. They harnessed and even performed a version of precarious living for the public. What these practices have shown is that people not only transformed a set of seemingly unstructured and disorganized practices *into work*, but they also put precarity *to work*.

My goal in this text, however, has not only been to outline the array of practices by which people in the boardwalk economy made ends meet. My goal has also been to better understand how the boardwalk's marketplace, as a social system, cohered and took shape to support a vastly diverse set of participants who managed very different configurations of precarity. In other words, how did this place, commonly described as unlike anywhere else in the world, come together? My central claim has been that when taken together, the collective practices to make precarity work served to transform a public space into a workplace, cultivate a community of workers, incorporate behaviors and experiences often seen as incompatible with work, and produce a generative social and economic world that fosters adaptive skills. The result was a supportive—subjectively defined, of course—social system that disrupted the dominant sociospatial order. I have called this social system a *subversive safety net*.

In chapter 2, we saw how people organized socially in ways that subverted city regulation and its purported goal for "equitable access." Instead of allowing the Public Expression Participant Permit Program to distribute spaces to individuals through a lottery draw, people exploited the conditions and characteristics of the lottery by playing a numbers game. They partnered together, formed networks, and traded in winnings. In doing so, people appropriated the public space to meet their own needs, with both social and material consequences.

People who lacked legal claims to citizenship could assert belonging, undermining immigration law by locating informal means to meet their needs, including access to work, housing, and leisure. Folks managing homelessness could gain "legitimate" social and economic ties to the boardwalk's marketplace, working as partners to those with more economic and social capital. And running contrary to portraits of precarious work that highlight a loss of collective participation, these workers filed a lawsuit that then changed the local ordinance. They drew on social networks, prior job training, and knowledge of prior legal action to change the conditions in which they worked. Doing so altered their material and social realities, as it allowed for new ways to establish control over property and practices. People began to form block communities, stabilizing the social and economic upheaval caused by an "egalitarian" distribution of space.

When Tim yelled, "We own this!" following the injunction of the ordinance, he asserted a collective reappropriation of public space. When Khaled sat back and proudly said, "They just don't want to see a Black man at the beach with his feet up," he defined his presence as an act of resistance in the social and racial order of urban America. From the perspective of these two participants, this was a way to wrest control back from the state and usher in new forms of claims making. Without romanticizing such agency, however, we also saw power dynamics and social hierarchies emerge and change form. People with access to social and economic resources often turned to those with fewer of them. Vulnerabilities were harnessed and exploited, exacerbating some of the precarious conditions people faced.

In chapter 3, we saw the subversive safety net grow more robust. Through daily interactions and meaning-making strategies, people cultivated a community of workers that offered forms of stability and security. People not only secured access to space, but financial assistance. They assisted one another with sales; they developed informal versions of paid time off and sick leave. They protected one another from disruptions, be they competition for income or punitive policies. They watched over one another's children, creating an informal version of childcare. The ability to stabilize their conditions from the ground up calls into question many dominant assumptions we hold about the benefits of formal employment, particularly low-wage labor, which increasingly lacks paid time off, sick leave, protection from punitive policies, and childcare. So, for all its many imperfections, the subversive safety net provided an alternative. Again, however, trust allowed for ongoing exclusion by protecting some at the expense of others. The line between "insiders" and "outsiders" was always fluid, but highly consequential.

In chapter 4, we saw how the subversive safety net supported people and practices often constructed as "undesirable." Drug and alcohol use gained new meaning as they were incorporated into the world of work on the boardwalk. Such practices structured time, defined relationships, and offered access to new identities. People who would far more often be approached as patients and clients found space to assert their autonomy to participate in the boardwalk marketplace as workers. Men like Rennie and RJ, both of whom were unhoused and suffered from differing levels of alcohol dependency, decentered their stigmatized identities to define themselves as workers.

As Rennie sat drinking alcohol and selling cardboard BUM SIGNS, he disrupted the presumed boundaries between work and vagrancy. Doing so offered him a right to space, albeit fragile, that he lacked elsewhere. For some, like Jorge, the boardwalk's subversive safety net offered a desirable opportunity out of dependency and into other forms of labor, undermining state policy that so often requires sobriety prior to employability. In cases where people lack private property to which they may retreat, the public sphere becomes a space of contestation over the right to be.[1] The subversive safety net afforded an opportunity to lay claim to space, and forced visitors into a beachfront confrontation with the dark side of global capitalism and neoliberal ideology that has left so many fending for themselves. But support is subjective, and the boardwalk had characteristics similar to those described by the sociologist Jacob Avery, who found that Atlantic City, New Jersey, represented an "enabling" habitat.[2] Being an active part of this social system could also exacerbate human suffering.

Finally, we saw how people navigated the precarious conditions of work, including those that emerged from the physical, legal, and social terrain. By peeling back the layers of "the sale," we saw how much work went into deciding what, when, where, and how to sell. The boardwalk, it turns out, was never a mere venue, but rather a productive and generative space that shaped the kind of activities possible and the kinds of identities people accessed. Participants' "talents" lay in learning to navigate this shifting terrain, and as a result, they produced a dynamic urban marketplace.

As Ousmane sewed a label into his merchandise stating PEACE, William hung his jewelry from inland wall space, and Marcus "sold" a pamphlet and handed a customer merchandise for "free," they subverted the state's conception of the Free Speech Zone and asserted their own right to work. Considering the additional layers of immigration law, as an immigrant like Ousmane waited for documentation that allowed him to work in the US, and racial segregation, as structurally marginalized workers laid claim to a beachfront swath of one of the country's wealthiest cities, these practices became assertions of citizenship and belonging. They challenged notions about who had a right to claim this stretch of California coastline and on what basis.

Not all the individual practices in which people engaged were subversive in their own right. Many people tried to follow the rules—some, like Umar, often advised tourists to put out cigarettes or conceal alcoholic beverages. But it is difficult to make sense of this social world by adding up individual practices, and I hope to have shown that a subversive safety net emerges as more than the sum of its parts. That is to say, as a *social system*, the boardwalk marketplace did undermine many of the social, economic, and legal barriers that restricted people's ability to meet their needs.

But while the subversive safety net is a collective accomplishment, it is not an unassailable one. For one, subversion becomes necessary only in the face of a state that has failed to provide the resources people require and that subjects them to exclusion and marginalization. In addition, we should be critical of the need to produce and enact "work" to access support, particularly when some versions of "support" only exacerbate the precarious conditions people face. Furthermore, even as people engage in acts of subversion, they do not dramatically transform broader structural conditions. Without access to the resources necessary to create sustained structural change, we should not romanticize marketplaces like the Venice boardwalk.

Many practices to produce the subversive safety net added to the immense vulnerability people experienced. Khaled, Marcus, Rennie, Chuck, Harold, and others all spent time in jail. Most participants received hefty fines at some point during their work, for everything from improper sunshade to selling impermissible goods. Men like Rennie, Sal, Chuck, and Benson engaged in harmful substance-use practices, and a year into my research, Anthony lost his life because of it. Umar was often away from his family, and given the issues of his long commute, he sometimes slept in his car rather than return home to his wife and children. Julian's RV was set on fire one night—an act he believed was rooted in the resentment of wealthy residents for his ability to claim housing on a public street.

For these reasons, the process of producing a subversive safety net deserves a critical eye. I am hopeful that readers will not ignore their own discomfort at confronting the circumstances in which so many here found themselves. Rather than presenting the subversive safety net as a laudable accomplishment, I have introduced it as a unifying concept through which to understand how the failures of government policy, gaps in the standard safety net, and inadequacies of wage labor physically manifest in the urban landscape. It allows us to understand more clearly how people collectively assert their own autonomy to address such failures, gaps, and inadequacies. In a society where the standard safety net is harshly inadequate, the alternative warrants close examination from the perspective of the people who weave it together each day.

A Pragmatic Approach

Umar told me about his own situation living in the San Gabriel Valley with his family, his wife, son, and daughter. He had fled political unrest to move to the US, and here they had a three-bedroom, two-bathroom house with rent for $1,600 a month. By the time he paid water, electricity, and gas, it was $2,000 a month, he said. His daughter was just about to graduate from high school, his son about to enter it. They had good schools in the area, he told me, but he had to navigate Los Angeles freeways. It was only about forty-five miles away from the boardwalk, he said, in a common Los Angeles lamentation that mileage had little to do with time. If it was before 5 a.m., he told me the trip could take forty-five minutes. But after 6 a.m. and on Friday evening, he said that it could take three hours. "That's too much," he told me. But Umar had to weigh the balance between cost of living and work options. He knew Los Angeles was much too expensive, and the commute was horrible. But at least this was work. He told me about a friend of his paying six hundred per month for rent in Michigan. "But there's no work," he said. "Here, much work, but expensive."

On another day, I sat in the back seat of an Uber rideshare, making my way back to Venice from Santa Monica. The driver chatted with me about work, and I told him about my research. "My brother Fred works out there," he said. "My brother is not exactly all there; he's got some issues." It turned out his brother was a quiet and rather isolated artist whose presence I knew well, but with whom I had never been able to speak. The driver told me a bit about their family, how they had grown up on the East Coast and moved a couple of times. His brother was a teenager when they got to Los Angeles, and he had already been dealing with mental health problems. He tried to run away and often wandered off. "I go up to him sometimes and ask if he wouldn't rather just get a job. Wouldn't you rather work somewhere where you can get some pay?" he recounted asking his brother. The driver then relayed Fred's response: he had said, "I can't work for anybody. So, making money for food is enough."

One crowded Saturday afternoon as I walked south, I saw two police officers pass me on their bikes as they headed in the opposite direction. I could see Michelle walking toward me. She stopped and put her arms out to give me a hug.

"How have you been?" she asked.

"Fine," I replied, "you?"

"I'm avoiding the cops," she told me, nodding a bit to the officers now north of us. "They keep harassing me," she said. She clarified that the officers had given her a ticket for selling a ten-dollar necklace. "There were a lot of people around the booth, and I got distracted," she told me. The ticket was for "selling a necklace." But she had told the officers that she had a "seller's permit," a permit that typically permits temporary sales and reports taxable income.

Confused by the relevance of a "seller's permit" to the boardwalk, I asked if that stopped the officers from issuing a fine for selling jewelry.

"No," Michelle said, but the officers asked her that if she had a "seller's permit," why wouldn't she go find another place to work? She laughed as she recounted her response to the officer's suggestion. "Where? Tell me where to go and I'll go there," she said. "I'm a single mom. I've got to take care of my son. I don't have a car. I take the bus everywhere. They think we make all this money, but I don't know where they get that. So, I don't pay rent on a store, but I do pay taxes. I'd love to have a little store, and then I'd pay taxes *and* rent, but I can't afford it. So, the only way is to be out here working, and the ticketing is making things worse."

Umar, Fred, and Michelle found themselves navigating vastly distinct circumstances. Umar's migration was sparked by geopolitical conflict, and he found himself supporting his family in the face of employment restrictions, job availability, and the cost of living. Fred managed mental health issues and believed himself unemployable, thus deciding on a form of work that allowed him to meet only the most basic of life's necessities. Michelle left professional employment in France to find success in America—a success that turned out to be more elusive than she had imagined. Like other participants, they each made a pragmatic choice to work on the boardwalk in the face of what they believed were inadequate alternatives. For all its imperfections, the subversive safety net still emerged as a safety net. But it was always produced in response to the inadequacies of the standard safety net, which is not only incomplete, but arguably inhumane. At times, the subversive safety net could be advantageous and fulfilling for people. At other times, it seemed only to play a role similar to other harm-reduction strategies.

Understanding cases like the boardwalk becomes increasingly necessary as we find ourselves in today's age of precarity. Our analyses can no longer afford to prioritize access to wage labor when wage labor no longer offers the kind of stability of the Fordist era. Furthermore, the sociopolitical landscape that undergirded Fordism has been replaced by neoliberal ideology and policy that increasingly places responsibility in the hands of individuals themselves. So, while governments increasingly rely on wage work to address social problems, wage work is increasingly ill equipped to do so. It forces people to subject themselves to the state; it too can be exploitative, abusive, and degrading.[3] For those who do access bits and pieces of the standard safety net like TANF and SSI, that same neoliberal ideology has stigmatized many such decisions. Even people barely scraping by on the boardwalk discussed their negative views of a "handout."

Many of the people working on the boardwalk, and laboring around the world, recognize (and even hope for) new arrangements between work and life, thereby disrupting dominant assumptions about the way work and life come together. As scholars of urban poverty have also shown, turning to both licit and illicit informal economies are often rational and pragmatic adaptations to the circumstances in which people find themselves.[4] To see such decisions from the perspective of the people who make them, it becomes particularly alarming to consider the alternatives.

When the free Thursday-night concert at the Santa Monica Pier ended, crowds of listeners who had covered the sand with their blankets and picnics began to disperse. I walked with friends along the concrete path, slowly making my way back home. I saw a man who seemed familiar in front of me, thin and hunched over. I did a double take when I passed him. "Marcus?" I said, a little alarmed at his transformation. He responded so quietly I could not make out what he said, but I may also have been so distracted by his appearance that I missed his response. His face seemed drained of color, his energy depleted. He told me that the cops had made it so tough for him to keep selling his goods, he was no longer able to work on the boardwalk. I knew he had ongoing conflicts with the police, but I hadn't quite realized the severity of the situation. He said things were rough, which was written all over his body. Unclear of what to do, I told him I wished him well. We parted ways in the crowd, and though I do not presume to know what happened, I never saw Marcus again.

Rennie, too, was removed from the boardwalk's community at times. One day, on my way to a grocery store two blocks inland, I passed him sitting on the curb. His head was down, and his hand had a loose grip on a sandwich.

"What's up?" I asked.

"I was kicked off [the boardwalk]," he told me.

The police had informed him that if he returned to the pathway, he risked fine and arrest. As we saw previously, Rennie often pushed the boundaries of the boardwalk's acceptable counterculture by attracting crowds of people more visibly linked to social problems like addiction and homelessness. By severing Rennie's ties to the boardwalk economy, the state removed his (albeit tenuous) status as a worker, the very status that allowed him some claim to be in this public space.[5] Few would argue that Rennie did not warrant a more comprehensive form of assistance and support, as his drinking behavior was quite clearly harmful. But that is not what he received. Instead, the punitive approach to public-space regulation simply removed him from the subversive safety net.

Extending the Case

There are many ways people informally meet their needs. Health-care is found through formal-informal hybrid systems, where people use "selective solidarity" to gain vital resources through restricted social networks.[6] Immigrant networks can offer loan services where access to financial institutions may be lacking.[7] Entire professions, like nurse practitioners, must expand their own roles to fill government inadequacies and meet patient needs.[8] Housing might be obtained through informal and "dis-posable ties,"[9] information exchanged through otherwise atom-ized employment networks,[10] goods and services through kinship networks.[11]

Furthermore, support systems take on additional character-istics when they are emplaced in the urban landscape. Economic and social stability can be obtained through "the underground" as poor communities produce robust, though insular, systems of economic exchange and social order to support and maintain them.[12] Economic and social support can emerge out of the physi-cal waste of capitalist consumption.[13] Neighborhood security can be obtained through the kind of ongoing interactions that sustain a local interaction order.[14] Street-level economies pop up where there is a "sustaining habitat" with access to pedestrians, food, and places to sleep.[15] "Enabling habitats" move beyond suste-nance to include physical proximity and access to vices that leave people to experience ongoing addiction and dependency.[16]

The subversive safety net can serve as a unifying concept with which to understand additional cases of urban informality, but it has distinguishing features designed to better understand the way a social system coheres, how it gains meaning for peo-ple, and with what consequences. First, the subversive safety net does not extend to cases of vending and busking that take place in an atomized fashion, such as selling loose cigarettes on the sidewalk. It is distinct from cases in which vendors are legally permitted through a restrictive credentialing process, including food trucks, subway performers, or even the vendors just a few miles north of Venice Beach who work on Santa Monica's heavily regulated Third Street Promenade. These practices often exclude many of the most marginalized in need of even the most imperfect safety net. It differs from the support networks of co-ethnics, or *paisanos*, who are often able to restrict participation to a select group of migrants; such networks shape power dynamics along particular axes of inequality, namely legal status.[17] A key tenet of the subversive safety net is its ability to capture folks managing such a wide breadth of experiences, such that a "struggling artist" would be apt to work alongside (and even collaborate with) an "unhoused person" selling garbage and struggling with mental health problems.

And while illicit vendors, including those selling restricted drugs, may develop social systems, they do so with quite distinct social consequences, power dynamics, and processes of identity formation than those who produce the subversive safety net. Violent sanctions were simply not effective on the boardwalk, precisely because social relations were often shaped by shifting state regulation and therefore always in flux. Power dynamics were fluid and dynamic, giving the economy its robustness and longevity.

I have also argued that the subversive safety net emerges as more than the sum of its parts, and it therefore differs from more isolated "acts of subversion," like sleeping on benches or skateboarding in a public park, and from informal safety nets that may emerge from the exchange of resources between otherwise dispersed networks of individuals. As stated at the start of this book, the subversive safety net is physically situated, collectively produced, always in production, and inherently dynamic.

I do, however, believe the subversive safety net acts as a conceptual tool with which to examine additional cases of urban informality. It requires that we ask what is being subverted, why, by whom, and with what consequences. It offers a way to examine how people—particularly those who have fallen through distinct cracks in our social, legal, and economic systems—come together to produce a coherent social system in which to make ends meet. It has the potential to tease apart the similarities and differences that may arise as people interact with different state apparatuses, since that dialogue is likely to shape new hierarchies and power dynamics. State-sponsored social safety nets (and their gaps) also differ, bringing different groups of people together to meet needs unmet elsewhere. Any subversive safety net will thereby take its shape through the gaps in local, national, and global policy. The concept also recognizes the dignity, autonomy, and claims-making strategies that people enact as they disrupt many dominant sociospatial norms. And finally, such disruption comes at different costs, shaping the reproduction of vulnerability and inequality we find in a subversive safety net. It is in identifying, contextualizing, and analyzing subversive safety nets—particularly as they are emplaced in the urban landscape—that we may be able to identify solutions to social problems that do not exacerbate the very challenges people face.

Precarity has offered a helpful lens, forcing us to reconsider how precarious work and precarious living intersect. This has the effect of shedding light on experiences beyond that of urban poverty, which I have argued captures only part of the experience of people on the boardwalk. Under the conditions of today's economic and sociopolitical context, the calculus of choosing precarious work versus a "real" job is simply not so clear. In the United States, for instance, we have witnessed the dismantling of a standard safety net and the general retreat of the state in its role to ensure a social wage that includes job security, healthcare benefits, pensions, and additional rights.[18] And the situation is here to stay. As Arne Kalleberg has stated, "Polarized and precarious employment systems result from the economic restructuring and removal of institutional protections that have been occurring since the 1970s; they are not merely temporary features of the business cycle that will self-correct once economic conditions improve. In particular, bad jobs are no longer vestigial but, rather, are a central—and in some cases growing—portion of employment in the United States."[19]

The paid workforce now consists of many contingent workers, whose jobs are uncertain and temporary.[20] The so-called flexibility of postindustrial America now defines the experiences of so many, seeping into our very conceptions of self.[21] We are encouraged to become mini businesses unto ourselves, moving from one gig to the next in what Allison Pugh has called a "tumbleweed society."[22] In the case of South Africa, for instance, Franco Barchiesi has noted that the link between employment and well-being is questionable, arguably because job creation (which increasingly includes jobs that lack a social wage) continues to be harnessed as the government response to social problems.[23]

What is particularly worrisome for folks who have fallen through the cracks in our social, economic, and legal systems is that such precariousness now defines the very professions that serve in support roles. For instance, human service agencies rely increasingly on contingency work, and research indicates that service workers recognize a significant cost in quality of treatment for clients.[24] It is imperative that we rethink how precarious work and other precarious life conditions intersect, including how different configurations of precarity may inform one another.

Moving Forward

People around the world will continue to turn to public spaces to make ends meet, dotting the urban landscape with endeavors for economic survival. But there continues to be a disconnect between the state's conception of public space and the way people are using it. When such a contradiction occurs, it is not uncommon for informal groups to be approached through punitive policies.[25] Yet such punitive policies to bring "order" to public spaces simply introduce new challenges to overcome.

When I rode my bike toward the boardwalk, I could see the LAPD vehicle parked by the food court where Rennie, Chuck, and Harold had recently been sleeping. I saw an encampment set up with crates and boxes, a couple of people wrapped up in sleeping bags. I got closer and saw Rennie, who was carrying a large, folded cardboard box, and Chuck, who hauled a large plastic bag with what appeared to be clothes and blankets. The officer sat in the driver's seat of the SUV and shined a light on the people sleeping. "I'm going to have to get out of the car," he said.

I approached Rennie and asked if the officers were making people move. "Not me," he said, "but everybody else is going to have to move. They're going to be pissed," he added.

I walked closer to the officer, who had by now stepped out of the car to shine his flashlight on a man and woman lying in the sleeping bags. They all began to argue, the sleeping-bag duo asserting that they were trying to make a living here and needed a place to sleep. The officer countered in a slightly mocking tone, "How exactly are you making a living?" Unable to prove how and otherwise unknown to the police officer, the pair picked up their belongings and left.

Because infractions in the boardwalk's marketplace were handled by the Los Angeles Police Department and not social services, people who were already vulnerable ended up in the criminal justice system. When the Pacific Division, which patrols the boardwalk, hired new officers for example, even tacit agreements were tested: a table that extended too far, an umbrella that was too large, a pendant that also served as a necklace, all ended up garnering fines. Those punitive policies were largely ineffective in quelling the kind of ongoing social issues that one found on the boardwalk; there was still visible homelessness, substance use, and mental health problems. When folks were arrested, most went right back to the boardwalk.

Rennie and Harold joked about their frequent stints in jail as a chance to eat peanut butter and jelly sandwiches and sleep indoors. Khaled and Marcus laughed and reminisced while they compared different prison environments. Sometimes people even relayed messages to one another as they overlapped in incarceration. People joked that the boardwalk was "all 5150 out here," a reference to the seventy-two-hour involuntary hold of a person having a mental health crisis. So-called homeless sweeps removed the visible signs of homelessness from the beach, but they also meant starting from scratch for many people whose belongings were confiscated.[26]

Democratic processes should also be reassessed for their ability to incorporate marginalized voices. For instance, when the boardwalk was declared by the city as a Free Speech Zone, it was constructed as a permissible market for expressive goods. But the city's conception of the space countered the way many used it—a conflict that also minimized and silenced many voices of those working in the marketplace. Specifically, the committees designed to brainstorm "solutions" to perceived "problems" were formed with only the city's conception in mind, thus allowing for representatives from only city-sanctioned roles: merchant, artist, performer, resident. Since commercial "vending" was not permitted, there was no vendor role. Nor were there any permitted roles for odd-job workers, whose labor was vital to the ongoing social world. Without representation of such key roles, the meetings themselves almost always devolved into arguments about who did, and did not, have a voice.

Tim tried to establish a role for unhoused folks, again defining himself as dedicated to ameliorating the experience of homelessness. When Betty took on the role of performer, an attending merchant became angry since she often vended commercial items. "I've also performed," Betty countered, again highlighting the blurred lines between different roles and the ease with which people moved between them. Regulating the boardwalk to limit participation to "artists and artisans" was a near impossibility. Few can define "art," let alone police its boundaries.[27] Instead, regulation ends up making arbitrary restrictions based largely on legal precedent rather than local context.

During the time of my research, Los Angeles had the most stringent anti-vending laws in the country. However, on September 17, 2018, Governor Jerry Brown signed the Safe Sidewalk Vending Act to end the criminalization of sidewalk vending in California. Instead, it permitted adoption of noncriminal laws to "protect public health, safety and welfare." Recognizing the need to use public sidewalks as workplaces is important. And by creating opportunities for people to do so, the state may limit some of the exploitation that comes from having only a few legal avenues to work. That said, formalizing vending practices is not likely to have equitable results. The creation of greater barriers to participation may allow for greater exploitation, particularly for folks who lack legal status, economic capital, documentation, and housing. There is likely to remain a need for opportunities with few formal barriers.

Since informal practices are an irreversible feature of globalized economies, scholars must continue to document and understand landscapes of informality, informal urbanism, and the sociospatial consequences.[28] We also need to examine the "rationality and dynamism" of such informal economies so we can design policies that are sensitive to people's needs.[29] This research echoes the call of additional scholars to better understand how people use space and seek solutions that can broker between marginalized groups and the state.[30]

Breaking Down

The sun approached the horizon, a picturesque warning of the city's requirement to "break down" the daily marketplace at sunset. It was only about 5:30; plenty of people still populated the pathway. And it was one more way the city's regulation fell out of step with those working here—that "closing time" would be demarcated by the sunset, an event that also drew potential customers. People lingered in newly purchased sweatshirts to view the deep-blue sky fade into a rich orange and, if they were lucky, a vivid magenta. Odd-job workers like Chuck reappeared after a midday absence to hover around vendors, pulling out bins and carts. Umar began removing his artwork from the grate to which it was adhered, piling it up on the table. Paul, Ricardo, and I all pulled the bins from under our own tables, though Ricardo soon left the job up to Chuck. We wrapped up items in plastic, laid them in their well-established configurations, unclamped the fabric from the tables, and folded it on top. A few spaces down, Khaled threw a folding table on its side, lifted it to the garbage can, and used the perch to fold his three tables easily. One by one, vendors, artists, and performers bound their daily displays into tight mobile carts. They used rope, bungee cords, and occasionally, balance and a prayer.

Rennie stood at the corner, wearing some kind of matted blond wig and holding onto a cylindrical paper bag. Benson walked briskly by me with his torso angled forward. Back from a day of relative inconspicuousness, he was clearly ready for business.

"Should I leave it here?" I asked as he passed by me, referring to my cart.

"Sure," he said without slowing his gait.

"I'm not working tomorrow," I told Paul.

"OK," he replied. "I'm not working Monday, though, so I'll see you Tuesday."

I relayed my Sunday absence to Umar as well.

"I'll save the spot," he said, "so if you come, cool; if not, no problem."

I turned to Leia and Manuel. "I'm not working tomorrow, but I should be back Monday."

"OK," Leia said, "let me know tomorrow afternoon about Monday so we'll save a space if you're coming."

As with every day, the ongoing actions of participants ensured that the workplace would be reconstructed by and for them when they arrived again.

"Are you leaving?" I heard a man say.

I looked up and saw Tim. "Oh my goodness!" I yelled, since I hadn't seen him in quite some time.

He told me he'd gone up to Michigan to work on a political campaign. Then he quickly listed a bunch of committees he was working with, though I failed to capture many of the details. He still swung his imaginary baseball bat as he talked excitedly. "I've got a ton of stuff to unload . . . but I'll have Rennie sell it the morning," he assured me. He returned to his question: "Why are you leaving? The best money comes now." As many vendors knew (though not all acted upon), it could be lucrative to push the limits of sunset. But it was just one more precarious situation, since LAPD could issue tickets for staying too late.

As participants in the boardwalk marketplace often discussed, the delineation of a sunset encouraged frequent resistance. And Tim, relatively privileged in his ability to pay a fine should he receive one, didn't seem too worried. He could exploit the fuzziness of a sunset to his benefit. After all, was the sunset marked by the official moment when the sun hit the horizon? Or the moment when the sun sank below it? Or, as typically invoked when people "watch the sunset," was it when the orange hues faded to darkness? Would the cops let you pass if it looked like you were *trying* to pack up as the sun descended? Like so much on the boardwalk, the uncertainty itself was both risk and asset.

Acknowledgments

This book developed with the feedback, suggestions, and support of many people. While I am certain I will not do them all justice, my hope is that all who contributed to this project over the years know that I am immensely appreciative.

As my graduate mentors, Stefan Timmermans and Vilma Ortiz offered ongoing insight, mentorship, and assurance throughout this project. I owe them both a great deal of gratitude. Stefan profoundly shaped the way I think about the social world. His encouragement to see and examine the puzzles and tensions that arise in everyday life influenced every aspect of this book, and I am so thankful for his guidance, suggestions, dinners, and the community of "Timmermaniacs" he forged. Vilma offered the kind of direction, feedback, and support one can only hope for in a mentor. I am so grateful to have had her in my corner all these years. Her sheer dedication and commitment to her students cultivated a community of scholars and friends that continues to humble me to this day.

I also thank the additional members of my dissertation committee, Ruben Hernández-Leon and Anastasia Loukaitou-Sideris, who offered thoughtful feedback and encouragement that helped shape the direction of the book project. From early training to professional development, the sociology faculty at UCLA undoubtedly impacted this project, and I owe additional thanks to

Jack Katz, David Halle, Edward Telles, Abigail Saguy, and many more for their insight and advice.

The most surprising and fulfilling outcome of graduate school has been the colleagues and friends who continue to inform my work and enrich my life. Forrest Stuart supported this project from beginning to end, and I am immensely grateful for the countless conversations, ongoing encouragement, and close friendship. I am so thankful to Elena Shih for infusing our moments together with her energy, advice, and encouragement. I thank John O'Brien for his support and unique way of reigniting the passion needed to keep this work going. I am grateful to Marie Berry for her support during some of the most challenging phases of our careers. I am thankful for the memories of writing and laughing alongside Anthony Ocampo and Lorenzo Perillo. Thank you also to Bobbi Ciriza Houtchens, who opened her home for writing, resting, and delicious meals.

I was fortunate to cross paths with so many wonderful people at UCLA. Whether through coursework, working groups, or informal conversations, their scholarship, advice, and encouragement helped me along the way. I am grateful to the members of the UCLA Ethnography Working Group. I thank Andrew Deener, whose excellent work on Venice informed my own. Thank you to the members of Vilma Ortiz's research group, who read draft after draft of my work, especially Silvia Zamora, Celia Lacayo, Irene Vega, Ariana Valle, Deisy Del Real, Karina Chavarria, Laura Enriquez, Casandra Salgado, Mirian Martinez-Aranda, Rocío R. García, and Carla Salazar Gonzalez. Following our time together at UCLA, Rocío Rosales, David Trouille, and Mike Deland each offered suggestions and support as we navigated writing our first book manuscripts. I am grateful to Alex Tate for her friendship and writing support, particularly as we both made Philadelphia our new home. I thank Amada Armenta for her support of the project and ongoing friendship. As I began my career, she welcomed me into a community of scholars and friends and has continued to offer her encouragement and thoughtful advice.

I presented parts of this project at numerous conferences and workshops, and I have benefited from the feedback of many scholars. In particular, I thank David Grazian, Annette Lareau, and Eli Anderson. I am also grateful for the ongoing support of Michaela Soyer, who read drafts, encouraged me to keep moving forward, and shared in some much-needed venting.

As I moved to my first faculty position at Penn State Abington, I could not have asked for a better group of colleagues with whom to begin my academic career. I thank Michael Bernstein, Jacob Benfield, Judith L. Newman, Russ Webster, Marissa Nicosia, and Alisha Walters. I am particularly grateful for my fellow sociologists Beth Montemurro, Elizabeth Hughes, and David Hutson, each of whom read chapters and proposal drafts. David's ongoing writing support and companionship pushed the project forward.

I am also fortunate to have joined the Sociology Department at Temple University in fall 2019, where I am surrounded by a group of talented and supportive faculty. Thank you to my colleagues Judith Levine, Rebecca Tesfai, Lu Zhang, Matt Wray, and Kevin Loughran, as well as graduate students Ewa Protasiuk and Andrew Chelius, who read portions of the book proposal and chapters and offered helpful feedback and advice. I also thank Kimberly Goyette and Dustin Kidd for their guidance and support as department chairs. I am so fortunate to have joined the department alongside Lauren D. Olsen, and I am certain that it was her feedback, support, and friendship that helped get me over those final hurdles.

This work was also made possible with the research support I received along the way, including the UCLA Diversity Initiative for Graduate Study in the Social Sciences grant, a UCLA Dissertation Completion Grant, the Consortium for Faculty Diversity Fellowship and Chau Mellon Postdoctoral Fellowship at Pomona College, a research fellowship in the Public Policy Lab at Temple University, and the Mellon Emerging Faculty Leaders award from the Institute of Citizens and Scholars.

I must also thank the editors who helped me along the way, including Kim Greenwell, Laura Portwood-Stacer, Kate Epstein, and Maura Roessner. I am particularly fortunate to have had the support and expertise of Elizabeth Branch Dyson and team, especially Mollie McFee and freelance copyeditor Johanna Rosenbohm, at the University of Chicago Press. Elizabeth's close engagement with my work ensured that our conversations were both informative and inspiring, and her guidance greatly impacted the development of this book. I also thank the many anonymous reviewers who read my work during this process and offered thoughtful feedback.

It is difficult to put into words how appreciative I am of my family and friends for holding me up throughout this project. Thank you to my parents, Sonia and Vincent Orrico, and my sister and brother-in-law, Cristina and Jim, for knowing when to read a draft or offer a hug. My family has always encouraged me to follow my interests and supported me to stay the course. I thank you all for the time and energy spent reviewing my work, advising me, and offering unwavering support. Marcus, thank you for over a decade of love, companionship, and reassurance. You kept me going with your reminders to eat, sleep, and get fresh air, and your feedback ensured that I infused these pages with the love for Venice that we both share. Tara, thank you for the years of vacations spent visiting me in LA. Warren, thank you for your insight, love, and commitment.

Finally, this project would be nothing without the people who wake up each day to work on the Venice boardwalk. I thank them all for sharing their stories and experiences with me. While life on the boardwalk is full of ups and downs, successes and struggles, it is my hope that these pages are full of the humanity I witnessed and critical of any instinct to turn a blind eye.

Notes

Chapter 1

1. See Kalleberg, *Good Jobs, Bad Jobs*, 2011.
2. In her study of garbage collectors in Brazil, Kathleen Millar presents and refutes many of these assumptions about the way work and life come together. See Millar, *Reclaiming the Discarded*, 2018.
3. Venkatesh, *American Project*, 2000; Contreras, *Stickup Kids*, 2012; Bourgois, *In Search of Respect*, 2003; Duck, *No Way Out*, 2015; Stuart, *Down, Out, and Under Arrest*, 2016.
4. Contreras, *Stickup Kids*, 2012; Duck, *No Way Out*, 2015; Bourgois, *In Search of Respect*, 2003.
5. Venkatesh, *Off the Books*, 2006, 17-18.
6. Rosales, *Fruteros*, 2020.
7. Mitchell Duneier found that the group of men he met selling written matter on Greenwich Village's Sixth Avenue had previously occupied Penn Station; many had moved together to Sixth Avenue as opportunities to sell written matter arose. See Duneier, *Sidewalk*, 1999, 123-32. Jacob Avery also built on Duneier's concept of a "sustaining habitat" to argue that some environments can become an "enabling" habitat. See Avery, "Surviving in America's Playground," 2014, 137-52, esp. 148; and Dunier, *Sidewalk*, 1999, 115-54, esp. 123.
8. Ferrell, *Empire of Scrounge*, 2006, 176. See also Gowan, *Hobos, Hustlers, and Backsliders*, 2010; Millar, *Reclaiming the Discarded*, 2018; and Duneier, *Sidewalk*, 1999.
9. Duneier, *Sidewalk*, 1999; Anderson, *Code of the Street*, 1999.
10. See Duck, *No Way Out*, 2015.

11. Contreras, *Stickup Kids*, 2012.

12. Levine, *Ain't No Trust*, 2013.

13. Rosales, *Fruteros*, 2020. Rocío Rosales finds that structural inequities produced by immigration policy and differential legal status can lead to informal work hierarchies and exploitation.

14. Ethnographic evidence indicates that ongoing police surveillance may spark behavioral adaptations by those being surveilled that negatively impact their own well-being. See Goffman, *On the Run*, 2014; and Stuart, *Down, Out, and Under Arrest*, 2016.

15. See Duck, *No Way Out*, 2015; Goffman, *On the Run*, 2014; Contreras, *Stickup Kids*, 2012; Venkatesh, *American Project*, 2000.

16. Much literature on urban informality focuses attention on immigrant groups whose experiences are often defined by shared ethnicity, homeland, and legal status. See, among others, Rosales, *Fruteros*, 2020; and Mukhija and Loukaitou-Sideris, *Informal American City*, 2014.

17. Sociological studies of illicit economic activity highlight the survival strategies of poor communities. See Bourgois, *In Search of Respect*, 2003; Contreras, *Stickup Kids*, 2012; Duck, *No Way Out*, 2015; Venkatesh, *American Project*, 2000; and Gowan, *Hobos, Hustlers, and Backsliders*, 2010.

18. Prior ethnographies portray street-level economic activity that is positioned to capture a public otherwise using the sidewalk for its role as a thoroughfare. See Duneier, *Sidewalk*, 1999; and Rosales, *Fruteros*, 2020.

19. Snyder, "Routes to the Informal Economy," 2004.

20. Lloyd, *Neo-Bohemia*, 2010; Deener, *Venice*, 2012.

21. Michèle de La Pradelle argues that the market in Carpentras, France, becomes "a sort of apparatus for producing equality of our highly diverse social material." See La Pradelle, *Market Day in Provence*, 2015, quotation on 177. While the boardwalk does blur the lines of social status, it is also clear that not all configurations of precarity are the same, and people are consistently vulnerable to shifting social hierarchies.

22. See Fine and Kleinman, "Rethinking Subculture," 1979.

23. For a typology of different adaptations to the boardwalk economy, see Deener, *Venice*, chap. 5.

24. See Duneier, *Sidewalk*, 1999.

25. See Silva, *Coming Up Short*, 2013; and Auyero, *Invisible in Austin*, 2015.

26. Shukaitis, "Recomposing Precarity," 2013.

27. Millar, "Toward a Politics of Precarity," 2017. Kathleen Millar's review of this concept emphasizes three different approaches to

precarity: condition (i.e., Pierre Bourdieu and precarity as labor condition), category (i.e., Guy Standing and precarity as socioeconomic category), and experience (i.e., Judith Butler and precariousness as a condition of human life).

28. Kallenberg, *Good Jobs, Bad Jobs*, 2011; Ross, *Nice Work If You Can Get It*, 2009.

29. Molé, "Precarious Subjects," 2010.

30. Kalleberg and Vallas, *Precarious Work*, 2018.

31. See Standing, *The Precariat*, 2014.

32. See Butler, *Precarious Life*, 2004.

33. Millar, "Toward a Politics of Precarity," 2017, 4.

34. An ongoing critique of the concept of precarity is that the focus on precarization as a post-Fordist process naturally takes Fordism as the starting point. Some have argued that to see precarity as a labor condition—one brought on by neoliberal policies and the end of the Fordist mode of production—is to see work only through the perspective of the wealthy nations. This critique argues that there may not be anything new per se, since people have long been laboring under precarious conditions around the world. In fact, it is likely that Fordism was the anomaly and not the other way around. For examples, see Neilson and Rossiter, "From Precarity to Precariousness," 2005; Millar, *Reclaiming the Discarded*, 2018; and Munck, "Precariat: View from the South," 2013.

35. Millar, "Toward a Politics of Precarity," 2017.

36. Hart, "Informal Economy," 1985.

37. Han, "Precarity, Precariousness, and Vulnerability," 2018. The belief that informal economies would diminish with development has largely been critiqued; scholars argue that informality is a direct result of global capitalism and does not decrease with development. See Sassen, *Global City*, 2001.

38. See, for example, Barchiesi, *Precarious Liberation*, 2011.

39. Millar, *Reclaiming the Discarded*, 2018.

40. Casas-Cortés, "Genealogy of Precarity," 2014, 207.

41. For an analysis of urban poverty through the lens of precariousness, see Duck, *No Way Out*, 2015.

42. See Millar, *Reclaiming the Discarded*, 2018.

43. I echo Kathleen Millar's interest in building on these approaches to harness precarity as a method of inquiry to explore the relationship between labor conditions and life. See Millar, "Toward a Politics of Precarity," 2017.

44. Steensland, "Cultural Categories and the Welfare State," 2006, 1314.

45. Lasky-Fink and Linos, "Improving Delivery of the Safety Net," 2022.

46. Arne Kalleberg argues that changes in the US economy beginning in the late 1970s led to increased polarization in job quality. While Kalleberg recognizes the subjective nature of "good" versus "bad" jobs, often hinging on a shifting set of characteristics from the state of the economy to personal expectations, he finds a general rubric for jobs regarded as "bad," which includes low wages, limited growth potential, lack of fringe benefits, lack of control, and lack of flexibility. Kalleberg, *Good Jobs, Bad Jobs*, 2011, 10.

47. Many informal economies develop strict social hierarchies on the basis of power and vulnerability. For example, Rocío Rosales shows how some workers garner power over others due to legal status. Rosales, *Fruteros*, 2020. Randol Contreras shows how violent acts maintain power dynamics. Contreras, *Stickup Kids*, 2012. Waverly Duck finds that violence is a patterned response to breaches in the local interaction order, so much so that it is relatively predictable and avoidable. Duck, *No Way Out*, 2015.

48. Attention to such tensions can also be seen in various chapters of Mukhija and Loukaitou-Sideris, *Informal American City*, 2014.

49. For a thorough analysis of Venice's multifaceted identity, see Deener, *Venice*, 2012.

50. For a detailed written and visual history of Venice, see Stanton, *Venice California*, 1993.

51. For a thorough discussion of suburbanization, see Jackson, *Crabgrass Frontier*, 1985.

52. Deener, *Venice*, 2012, 44-85. Andrew Deener argues that while demographic shifts took place in the Oakwood section of Venice, the public identity of the area has remained Black. This is due largely to the history of racial segregation and subsequent community building in the area, leading to what Deener calls "collective visibility" (60).

53. Kalleberg, *Good Jobs, Bad Jobs*, 2011.

54. Murolo and Chitty, *Folks Who Brought You the Weekend*, 2018; Edgell, *Sociology of Work*, 2012.

55. For an overview of policies and practices that have privileged white Americans, see Katznelson, *When Affirmative Action Was White*, 2006.

56. Jackson, *Crabgrass Frontier*, 1985.

57. For an analysis that complicates the concept of suburbia, see Fishman, *Bourgeois Utopias*, 1987.

58. Lipton, *Holy Barbarians*, 1959, 15. A Polish immigrant to Chicago, Lawrence Lipton was a writer and poet who moved to Venice

and emerged as a prominent member of Southern California's Beat generation. He wrote *The Holy Barbarians* to capture the cultural moment happening on Venice Beach.

59. Lloyd, *Neo-Bohemia*, 2010, 63.

60. Lloyd, 2010. For an account of Venice's beatniks, see Maynard, *Venice West*, 1991.

61. Peralta, *Dogtown and Z-Boys*, 2002. Produced by Agi Orsi and directed by Stacy Peralta, the 2001 documentary *Dogtown and Z-Boys* follows the emergence of extreme skateboarding as it evolved alongside the innovative surf culture of Venice and Santa Monica. While many surfers navigated the remains of Pacific Ocean Park, the dilapidated pier technically located within the Ocean Park neighborhood of Santa Monica on Venice's northern border, the subculture and moniker Dogtown are largely associated with Venice.

62. Beveridge and Weber, "Race and Class in the Developing Metropolises," 2003, 61; Sabagh and Bozorgmehr, "From 'Give Me Your Poor,'" 2003, 105.

63. Deener, *Venice*, 2012.

64. Sabagh and Bozorgmehr, "From 'Give Me Your Poor,'" 2003, 107.

65. Deener, *Venice*, 2012.

66. Wolch and Dear, *Malign Neglect*, 1993, 56.

67. Gladstone and Fainstein, "New York and Los Angeles Economies," 2003, 88.

68. Wolch and Dear, *Malign Neglect*, 1993.

69. Wolch and Dear. For a recent study on the differing effects of deinstitutionalization, see Gong, *Sons, Daughters, and Sidewalk Psychotics*, 2024.

70. Gong, 148.

71. Mitchell, *Mean Streets*, 2020, 29.

72. Loukaitou-Sideris and Ehrenfeucht, *Sidewalks*, 2009.

73. Duneier, *Sidewalk*, 1999, 143-44. Mitchell Duneier discusses the characteristics of a habitat capable of sustaining a group of unhoused men. He notes that the "density of people, convergence of transportation lines carrying many persons from various parts of the city, people willing to make donations, cheap or free food, places to sleep," and various other resources that support an economy is written matter. Duneier also shows how part of the social cohesion results from prior shared history. See also n7, above.

74. Stuart, *Down, Out, and Under Arrest*, 2016.

75. For an overview of vehicular homelessness in Los Angeles, see Giamarino, Blumenberg, and Brozen, "Who Lives in Vehicles?," 2002.

76. Deener, *Venice*, 2012, 193.

77. For a historical overview of Los Angeles vending, including a list of vending restrictions, see Loukaitou-Sideris and Ehrenfeucht, *Sidewalks*, 2009.

78. Gottlieb et al., *Next Los Angeles*, 2006.

79. Gladstone and Fainstein, "New York and Los Angeles Economies," 2003.

80. Gottlieb et al., *Next Los Angeles*, 2006.

81. The article by Marilyn Martinez, "Deadly Venice Gang War Turns to Race War," was published on the front page of the *Venice-Marina News*, November 25, 1993, partially reprinted in Umemoto, *Truce*, 2006, 108.

82. For an analysis of Venice's "gang war" and the role of race and racialization in shaping urban conflict, see Umemoto, *Truce*, 2006.

83. "L.A.'s most visible": Deener, *Venice*, 2012, 32.

84. Lloyd, *Neo-Bohemia*, 2010. On enterprises eager to exploit such qualities, see Zukin, *Naked City*, 2010.

85. Hernandez, "Snapchat's Disappearing Act," 2019.

86. Between 2019 and 2020, the point-in-time homeless population in Venice grew from 1,118.2 to 1,669.2, a 50 percent increase. The 2020 count is also more than double that of 2018, which was 726.4. See Los Angeles Homeless Services Authority, "Homeless Count by City/Community" (select Venice under "Search or Select a Community/City").

87. For a comprehensive analysis of the tensions that arise between Venice's distinct public identities, see Deener, *Venice*, 2012.

88. Stuart, *Down, Out, and Under Arrest*, 2016, 2.

89. See Timmermans and Tavory, *Data Analysis in Qualitative Research*, 2022.

90. See Orrico, "Doing Intimacy," 2015.

Chapter 2

1. On the public-space marketplace as a daily social accomplishment, see La Pradelle, *Market Day in Provence*, 2015.

2. Mitchell, *Mean Streets*, 2020.

3. For examples, see Rosales, *Fruteros*, 2020; Duck, *No Way Out*, 2015; and Contreras, *Stickup Kids*, 2012.

4. Deener, *Venice*, 2012.

5. For an overview of everyday resistance, see Johansson and Vinthagen, *Conceptualizing "Everyday Resistance,"* 2019.

6. Though I had doubts about the condo, I was able to see it with my own eyes when Tim and I stopped by on our way to downtown Los

Angeles. It was clearly occupied, though his brother was not at home. It bore the marks of a bachelor pad, relatively untidy with curtains drawn and a leftover pizza box on the counter. Tim clearly knew his way around the place, and just did some basic review of the place—including throwing the pizza box in the trash—before we left.

7. See Rosales, *Fruteros*, 2020.

8. See Rosales.

9. See Duneier, *Sidewalk*, 1999; Gowan, *Hobos, Hustlers, and Backsliders*, 2010; and Stuart, *Down, Out, and Under Arrest*, 2016.

10. Duneier, *Sidewalk*, 1999.

11. See *Dowd v. City of L.A.*, 28 F. Supp. 3d 1019 (C.D. Cal. 2010). On October 21, 2010, the court granted in part the plaintiffs' motion for a preliminary injunction and enjoined the amplified sound ban as well as the permit and lottery system set forth in LAMC §42.15.3.

12. See Venkatesh, *American Project*, 2000; Duck, *No Way Out*, 2015; and Rosales, *Fruteros*, 2020.

13. See Duneier, *Sidewalk*, 1999; and Deener, *Venice*, 2012.

Chapter 3

1. Garfinkel, "Conception of 'Trust,'" 1963.

2. Watson, "Constitutive Practices and Garfinkel's Notion," 2009.

3. Fine, *Tiny Publics*, 2012; Duck, *No Way Out*, 2015.

4. Levine, *Ain't No Trust*, 2013.

5. Desmond, *Evicted*, 2016.

6. Duck, *No Way Out*, 2015.

7. See Kollock, "Emergence of Exchange Structures," 1994.

8. For more on trust as an interactional process, see Weber and Carter, *Social Construction of Trust*, 2003.

Chapter 4

1. Avery, "Surviving in America's Playground," 2014, 137–52, esp. 148. See also chap. 1, n7, above.

2. Douglas, *Constructive Drinking*, 1987.

3. On choice of substance, see McKay et al., "Their Type of Drugs," 2012. On method, see Slavin, "Drugs, Space, and Sociality," 2004.

4. Lyons, Emslie, and Hunt, "Staying 'In the Zone,'" 2014; Lyons and Willott, "Alcohol Consumption, Gender Identities," 2008; Peralta, "Alcohol Allows You," 2008, Peralta and Jauk, "Brief Feminist Review of Treatment," 2011.

5. On violence, see Tryggvesson, "Ambiguous Excuse," 2004. On increased sexual freedom, see Cohen and Lederman, "Navigating the Freedom of College," 1998.

6. Millar, *Reclaiming the Discarded*, 2018.

7. On alcohol and drug use in public spaces viewed through the lens of disorder and consequently leading to punitive measures, see Dixon, Levine, and McAuley, "Locating Impropriety," 2006; and Loukaitou-Sideris and Ehrenfeucht, *Sidewalks*, 2009.

8. Adler and Adler, "Dry with a Wink," 1983.

9. Dixon, Levine, and McAuley, "Locating Impropriety," 2006, 201-2.

10. Anderson, *Place on the Corner*, 1978; Anderson, *Code of the Street*, 1999; Britton, "My Regular Spot," 2008; Trouille, *Fútbol in the Park*, 2021.

11. Rosen and Venkatesh, "'Perversion' of Choice," 2008. The authors draw from a case study of sex workers to argue that participation can be a rational and agential choice that runs counter to dominant assumptions of sex workers as victims. "Bounded rationality": Rosen and Venkatesh, "Perversion of Choice," 2008, 425. Limited by structural forces that marginalize people, they turn to work that provides *"just enough"* (418; italics in the original). As Rosen and Venkatesh argue, it "satisfices" (425).

12. Bourgois, *In Search of Respect*, 2003; Bourgois and Schonberg, *Righteous Dopefiend*, 2009; Gowan, *Hobos, Hustlers, and Backsliders*, 2010.

13. See Roy, "Banana Time," 1959-1960.

14. See Bourgois and Schonberg, *Righteous Dopefiend*, 2009; Venkatesh, *American Project*, 2000; Deener, *Venice*, 2012; Duneier, *Sidewalk*, 1999; and Gowan, *Hobos, Hustlers, and Backsliders*, 2010.

15. Millar, *Reclaiming the Discarded*, 2018, 99.

16. Deener, *Venice*, 2012.

17. Stuart, *Down, Out, and Under Arrest*, 2016.

18. Exec. Order No. 12,564.

19. See Anderson, *Code of the Street*, 1999; and Duneier, *Sidewalk*, 1999.

20. The bootstrap myth is often linked to the "rags to riches" story of Horatio Alger; it has also been largely critiqued. Quart, *Bootstrapped*, 2022.

21. Millar, *Reclaiming the Discarded*, 2018.

22. See Gowan, *Hobos, Hustlers, and Backsliders*, 2010.

Chapter 5

1. Wherry, *Culture of Markets*, 2012.

2. See Deener, *Venice*, 2012.

3. Deener.

4. Deener.

5. Lien, Dave, and Agrawal, "Snapchat Firm Makes History," 2017.

6. This statement refers to the general acceptance that products and merchandise are fair game. There are some specific cases in which public figures have received and expect greater protection over their own images and activities—for example, the musician Harry Perry won the right to sell products that included his own image. It would not be acceptable for other vendors to sell his image; they could, however, adopt the same *idea* and sell their own image.

Chapter 6

1. Mitchell, "Annihilation of Space by Law," 1997; Mitchell, *Right to the City*, 2003.

2. Avery, "Surviving in America's Playground," 2014, 137-52, esp. 148. See also chap. 1, n7, above.

3. Millar, *Reclaiming the Discarded*, 2018.

4. See, for example, Venkatesh, *Off the Books*, 2006; Contreras, *Stickup Kids*, 2012; and Duck, *No Way Out*, 2015.

5. See Hatton, *Coerced*, 2020.

6. Raudenbush, *Health Care Off the Books*, 2020, 25.

7. Rosales, *Fruteros*, 2020.

8. Trotter, *More Than Medicine*, 2020.

9. Desmond, "Disposable Ties and the Urban Poor," 2012, 1296.

10. Hondagneu-Sotelo, "Regulating the Unregulated?," 1994.

11. Stack, *All Our Kin*, 1974.

12. Venkatesh, *Off the Books*, 2006.

13. Gowan, *Hobos, Hustlers, and Backsliders*, 2010; Millar, *Reclaiming the Discarded*, 2018.

14. Duck, *No Way Out*, 2015.

15. Duneier, *Sidewalk*, 1999, Dunier, *Sidewalk*, 1999, 115-54, esp. 123. See also chap. 1, n7, above.

16. Avery, "Surviving in America's Playground," 2014, 137-52, esp. 148. See also chap. 1, n7, above.

17. Rosales, *Fruteros*, 2020.

18. Sassen, *Global City*, 2001, 339-40.

19. Kalleberg, *Good Jobs, Bad Jobs*, 2011, 15.

20. Newman and Winston, *Reskilling America*, 2016; Bureau of Labor Statistics (2017).

21. Silva, *Coming Up Short*, 2013.

22. Pugh, *Tumbleweed Society*, 2015.

23. Barchiesi, *Precarious Liberation*, 2011.

24. Hyde, "Does Contingency Work Compromise?," 2020.

25. Rios, "Learning from Informal Practices," 2014.

26. For more on the nature of such sweeps, see Deener's discussion of "discontinuity techniques": Deener, *Venice*, 2012, 98-108, quotation on 98.

27. Such difficulties were regularly covered in local and national news media. See, for example, Karp, "Is It Art?," 2012.

28. Loukaitou-Sideris and Mukhija, "Conclusion," 2014; Valenzuela, "Regulating Day Labor," 2014.

29. Ward, "Reproduction of Informality," 2014.

30. See, for example, Rios, "Learning from Informal Practices," 2014.

Works Cited

Adler, Patricia A., and Peter Adler. "Dry with a Wink: Normative Clash and Social Order." *Urban Life* 12, no. 2 (1983): 123-39.

Anderson, Elijah. *Code of the Street: Decency, Violence, and the Moral Life of the Inner City.* New York: W. W. Norton, 1999.

———. *A Place on the Corner.* Chicago: University of Chicago Press, 1978.

Auyero, Javier, ed. *Invisible in Austin: Life and Labor in an American City.* Austin: University of Texas Press, 2015.

Avery, Jacob. "Surviving in America's Playground: Informal Sustenance Strategies among the Chronically Unhoused." In *The Informal American City: Beyond Taco Trucks and Day Labor*, edited by Vinit Mukhija, Anastasia Loukaitou-Sideris, 137-52. Cambridge, MA: MIT Press, 2014.

Barchiesi, Franco. *Precarious Liberation: Workers, the State, and Contested Social Citizenship in Postapartheid South Africa.* Albany: State University of New York Press, 2011.

Beveridge, Andrew A., and Susan Weber. "Race and Class in the Developing New York and Los Angeles Metropolises: 1940-2000." In *New York and Los Angeles*, edited by David Halle. Chicago: University of Chicago Press, 2003.

Bourgois, Philippe. *In Search of Respect.* 2nd ed. Cambridge: Cambridge University Press, 2003.

Bourgois, Philippe, and Jeffrey Schonberg. *Righteous Dopefiend.* Berkeley: University of California Press, 2009.

Britton, Marcus. "'My Regular Spot': Race and Territory in Urban Public Space." *Journal of Contemporary Ethnography* 37, no. 4 (2008): 442-68.

Butler, Judith. *Precarious Life: The Powers of Mourning and Violence.* London: Verso, 2004.

Casas-Cortés, Maribel. "A Genealogy of Precarity: A Toolbox for Rearticulating Fragmented Social Realities in and out of the Workplace." *Rethinking Marxism* 26, no. 2 (2014): 206-26.

Cohen, Deborah J., and Linda C. Lederman. "Navigating the Freedom of College Life: Students Talk about Alcohol, Gender, and Sex." In *Women and AIDS: Negotiating Safer Practices, Care, and Representation,* edited by Nancy L. Roth and Linda K. Fuller, 101-26. New York: Haworth Press, 1998.

Contreras, Randol. *The Stickup Kids: Race, Drugs, Violence, and the American Dream.* Berkeley: University of California Press, 2012.

Deener, Andrew. *Venice: A Contested Bohemia in Los Angeles.* Chicago: University of Chicago Press, 2012.

Desmond, Matthew. "Disposable Ties and the Urban Poor." *American Journal of Sociology* 117 no. 5 (2012): 1295-1335.

———. *Evicted: Poverty and Profit in the American City.* New York: Broadway Books, 2016.

Dixon, John, Mark Levine, and Rob McAuley. "Locating Impropriety: Street Drinking, Moral Order, and the Ideological Dilemma of Public Space." *Political Psychology* 27, no. 2 (2006): 187-206.

Douglas, Mary. *Constructive Drinking: Perspectives on Drink from Anthropology.* Cambridge: Cambridge University Press, 1987.

Duck, Waverly. *No Way Out: Precarious Living in the Shadow of Poverty and Drug Dealing.* Chicago: University of Chicago Press, 2015.

Duneier, Mitchell. *Sidewalk.* New York: Farrar, Straus and Giroux, 1999.

Edgell, Stephen. *The Sociology of Work: Continuity and Change in Paid and Unpaid Work.* 2nd ed. London: Sage, 2012.

Farrell, Jeff. *Empire of Scrounge: Inside the Urban Underground of Dumpster Diving, Trash Picking, and Street Scavenging.* New York: NYU Press, 2006.

Fine, Gary Alan. *Tiny Publics: A Theory of Group Action and Culture.* New York: Russell Sage Foundation, 2012.

Fine, Gary Alan, and Sherryl Kleinman. "Rethinking Subculture: An Interactionist Analysis." *American Journal of Sociology* 85, no. 1 (1979): 1-20.

Fishman, Robert. *Bourgeois Utopias.* New York: Basic Books, 1987.

Garfinkel, Harold. "A Conception of, and Experiments with, 'Trust' as a Condition of Stable Concerted Actions." In *Motivation and Social Interaction: Cognitive Determinants,* edited by O. J. Harvey, 187-238. New York: Ronald Press, 1963.

Giamarino, Christopher, Evelyn Blumenberg, and Madeline Brozen. "Who Lives in Vehicles and Why? Understanding Vehicular Homelessness in Los Angeles." *Housing Policy Debate* 34, no. 1 (2022): 25–38.

Gladstone, David L., and Susan S. Fainstein. "The New York and Los Angeles Economies." In *New York and Los Angeles*, edited by David Halle, 79–98. Chicago: University of Chicago Press, 2003.

Goffman, Alice. *On the Run*. Chicago: University of Chicago Press, 2014.

Gong, Neil. *Sons, Daughters, and Sidewalk Psychotics: Mental Illness and Homelessness in Los Angeles*. Chicago: University of Chicago Press, 2024.

Gottlieb, Robert, Regina Freer, Mark Vallianatos, and Peter Dreier. *The Next Los Angeles: The Struggle for a Livable City*. Berkeley: University of California Press, 2006.

Gowan, Theresa. *Hobos, Hustlers, and Backsliders: Homeless in San Francisco*. Minneapolis: University of Minnesota Press, 2010.

Han, Clara. "Precarity, Precariousness, and Vulnerability." *Annual Review of Anthropology* 47, no. 1 (2018): 331–43.

Hart, Keith. "The Informal Economy." *Cambridge Anthropology* 10, no. 2 (1985): 54–58.

Hatton, Erin. *Coerced: Work under Threat of Punishment*. Oakland: University of California Press, 2020.

Hernandez, Daniel. "Snapchat's Disappearing Act Leaves Venice Beach Searching for Its Future." *New York Times*, August 23, 2019.

Hondagneu-Sotelo, Pierrette. "Regulating the Unregulated? Domestic Workers' Social Networks." *Social Problems* 41, no. 1 (1994): 50–64.

Hyde, C. A. "Does Contingency Work in Human Service Agencies Compromise Practice and Practice Ethics? An Exploratory Study." *Ethics and Social Welfare* 14, no. 1 (2020): 39–51.

Jackson, Kenneth. *Crabgrass Frontier: The Suburbanization of the United States*. Oxford: Oxford University Press, 1985.

Johansson, Anna, and Stellan Vinthagen. *Conceptualizing "Everyday Resistance": A Transdisciplinary Approach*. New York: Routledge, 2019.

Kalleberg, Arne L. *Good Jobs, Bad Jobs: The Rise of Polarized and Precarious Employment Systems in the United States, 1970s to 2000s*. New York: Russell Sage Foundation, 2011.

Kalleberg, Arne L., and Steven P. Vallas, eds. *Precarious Work*. Bingley, UK: Emerald Publishing, 2018.

Karp, Hannah. "Is It Art? On Venice Beach, Police Can Make the Call." *Wall Street Journal*, November 25, 2012.

Katznelson, Ira. *When Affirmative Action Was White: An Untold History of Racial Inequality in Twentieth-Century America*. New York: W. W. Norton, 2006.

Kollock, Peter. "The Emergence of Exchange Structures: An Experimental Study of Uncertainty, Commitment, and Trust." *American Journal of Sociology* 100, no. 2 (1994): 313–45.

La Pradelle, Michèle de. *Market Day in Provence*. Translated by Amy Jacobs. Chicago: University of Chicago Press, 2015.

Lasky-Fink, Jessica, and Elizabeth Linos. "Improving Delivery of the Social Safety Net: The Role of Stigma." HKS Faculty Research Working Paper Series RWP22-022, November 2022.

Levine, Judith. *Ain't No Trust: How Bosses, Boyfriends, and Bureaucrats Fail Low-Income Mothers and Why It Matters*. Berkeley: University of California Press, 2013.

Lien, Tracey, Paresh Dave, and Nina Agrawal. "Snapchat Firm Makes History in Stock Market Debut." *Los Angeles Times*, March 2, 2017.

Lipton, Lawrence. *The Holy Barbarians*. New York: Julian Messner, 1959.

Lloyd, Richard. *Neo-Bohemia: Art and Commerce in the Postindustrial City*. 2nd ed. New York: Routledge, 2010.

Los Angeles Homeless Services Authority. "Homeless Count by City/Community, 2016–2022." Last accessed August 12, 2024. https://www.lahsa.org/data?id=54-homeless-count-by-city-community.

Loukaitou-Sideris, Anastasia, and Renia Ehrenfeucht. *Sidewalks: Conflict and Negotiation over Public Space*. Cambridge, MA: MIT Press, 2009.

Loukaitou-Sideris, Anastasia, and Vinit Mukhija. "Conclusion: Deepening Our Understanding of Informal Urbanism." In *The Informal American City: Beyond Taco Trucks and Day Labor*, edited by Vinit Mukhija and Anastasia Loukaitou-Sideris, 295–304. Cambridge, MA: MIT Press, 2014.

Lyons, Antonia C., Carol Emslie, and Kate Hunt. "Staying 'In the Zone' but Not Passing the 'Point of No Return': Embodiment, Gender and Drinking in Mid-life." *Sociology of Health & Illness* 36, no. 2 (2014): 264–77.

Lyons, Antonia C., and Sara A. Willott. "Alcohol Consumption, Gender Identities and Women's Changing Social Positions." *Sex Roles* 59 (2008): 694–712.

Maynard, John Arthur. *Venice West: The Beat Generation in Southern California*. New Brunswick, NJ: Rutgers University Press, 1991.

McKay, Tara, Bryce McDavitt, Sheba George, and Matt G. Mutchler. "'Their Type of Drugs': Perceptions of Substance Use, Sex and

Social Boundaries among Young African American and Latino Gay and Bisexual Men." *Culture, Health & Sexuality* 14, no. 10 (2012): 1183-96.

Millar, Kathleen M. *Reclaiming the Discarded: Life and Labor on Rio's Garbage Dump*. Durham, NC: Duke University Press, 2018.

———. "Toward a Critical Politics of Precarity." *Sociology Compass* 11, no. 6 (2017): 1-11.

Mitchell, Don. "The Annihilation of Space by Law: The Roots and Implications of Anti-homeless Laws in the United States." *Antipode* 29, no. 3 (1997): 303-35.

———. *Mean Streets: Homelessness, Public Space, and the Limits of Capital*. Athens: University of Georgia Press, 2020.

———. *The Right to the City*. New York: Guilford, 2003.

Molé, N. J. "Precarious Subjects: Anticipating Neoliberalism in Northern Italy's Workplace." *American Anthropologist* 112, no. 1 (2010): 38-53.

Mukhija, Vinit, and Anastasia Loukaitou-Sideris, eds. *The Informal American City: Beyond Taco Trucks and Day Labor*. Cambridge, MA: MIT Press, 2014.

Munck, Ronaldo. "The Precariat: A View from the South." *Third World Quarterly* 34, no. 5 (2013): 747-62.

Murolo, Priscilla, and A. B. Chitty. *From the Folks Who Brought You the Weekend: A Short, Illustrated History of Labor in the United States*. New York: New Press, 2018.

Neilson, Brett, and Ned Rossiter. "From Precarity to Precariousness and Back Again: Labour, Life and Unstable Networks." *Fibreculture Journal* 5 (2005).

Newman, K., and H. Winston. *Reskilling America: Learning to Labor in the Twenty-First Century*. New York: Henry Holt, 2016.

Orrico, Laura A. "'Doing Intimacy' in a Public Market: How the Gendered Experience of Ethnography Reveals Situated Social Dynamics." *Qualitative Research* 15, no. 4 (2015): 473-88.

Peralta, Robert L. "'Alcohol Allows You to Not Be Yourself': Toward a Structured Understanding of Alcohol Use and Gender Difference among Gay, Lesbian, and Heterosexual Youth." *Journal of Drug Issues* 38, no. 2 (2008): 373-99.

Peralta, Robert L., and Daniela Jauk. "A Brief Feminist Review and Critique of the Sociology of Alcohol-Use and Substance-Abuse Treatment Approaches." *Sociology Compass* 5, no. 10 (2011): 882-97.

Peralta, Stacy, dir. *Dogtown and Z-Boys*. Sony Pictures Classics, 2002.

Pugh, Alison. *The Tumbleweed Society: Working and Caring in an Age of Insecurity.* Oxford: Oxford University Press, 2015.

Quart, Alissa. *Bootstrapped: Liberating Ourselves from the American Dream.* New York: Harper Collins, 2023.

Raudenbush, Danielle. *Health Care Off the Books: Poverty, Illness, and Strategies for Survival in Urban America.* Berkeley: University of California Press, 2020.

Rios, Michael. "Learning from Informal Practices: Implications for Urban Design." In *The Informal American City: Beyond Taco Trucks and Day Labor,* edited by Vinit Mukhija, Anastasia Loukaitou-Sideris, 173–92. Cambridge, MA: MIT Press, 2014.

Rosales, Rocío. *Fruteros: Street Vending, Illegality, and Ethnic Community in Los Angeles.* Berkeley: University of California Press, 2020.

Rosen, Eva, and Sudhir Alladi Venkatesh. "A 'Perversion' of Choice: Sex Work Offers Just Enough in Chicago's Urban Ghetto." *Journal of Contemporary Ethnography* 37, no. 4 (2008): 417–41.

Ross, Andrew. *Nice Work If You Can Get It: Life and Labor in Precarious Times.* New York: NYU Press, 2009.

Roy, Donald F. "'Banana Time': Job Satisfaction and Informal Interaction." *Human Organization* 18, no. 4 (1959–1960): 158–68.

Sabagh, Georges, and Mehdi Bozorgmehr. "From 'Give Me Your Poor' to 'Save Our State': New York and Los Angeles as Immigrant Cities and Regions." In *New York and Los Angeles,* edited by David Halle, 99–123. Chicago: University of Chicago Press, 2003.

Sassen, Saskia. *The Global City: New York, London, Tokyo.* 2nd ed. Princeton, NJ: Princeton University Press, 2001.

Shukaitis, S. "Recomposing Precarity: Notes on the Laboured Politics of Class Composition." *Ephemera: Theory and Politics in Organization* 13, no. 3 (2013): 641–58.

Silva, Jennifer M. *Coming Up Short: Working-Class Adulthood in an Age of Uncertainty.* Oxford: Oxford University Press, 2013.

Slavin, Sean. "Drugs, Space, and Sociality in a Gay Nightclub in Sydney." *Journal of Contemporary Ethnography* 33, no. 3 (2004): 265–95.

Snyder, Karrie Ann. "Routes to the Informal Economy in New York's East Village: Crisis, Economics, and Identity." *Sociological Perspectives* 47, no. 2 (2004): 215–40.

Stack, Carol. *All Our Kin: Strategies for Survival in a Black Community.* New York: Basic Books, 1974.

Standing, Guy. *The Precariat: The New Dangerous Class.* London: Bloomsbury, 2014.

Stanton, Jeffrey. *Venice California: "Coney Island of the Pacific."* Los Angeles: Donahue, 1993.

Steensland, Brian. "Cultural Categories and the American Welfare State: The Case of Guaranteed Income Policy." *American Journal of Sociology* 111, no. 5 (2006): 1273-1326.

Stuart, Forrest. *Down, Out, and Under Arrest: Policing and Everyday Life in Skid Row.* Chicago: University of Chicago Press, 2016.

Timmermans, Stefan, and Iddo Tavory. *Data Analysis in Qualitative Research: Theorizing with Abductive Analysis.* Chicago: University of Chicago Press, 2022.

Trotter, LaTonya J. *More Than Medicine: Nurse Practitioners and the Problems They Solve for Patients, Health Care Organizations, and the State.* Ithaca, NY: Cornell University Press, 2020.

Trouille, David. *Fútbol in the Park: Immigrants, Soccer, and the Creation of Social Ties.* Chicago: University of Chicago Press, 2021.

Tryggvesson, Kalle. "The Ambiguous Excuse: Attributing Violence to Intoxication—Young Swedes about the Excuse Value of Alcohol." *Contemporary Drug Problems* 31, no. 2 (2004): 231-61.

Umemoto, Karen. *The Truce: Lessons from an L.A. Gang War.* Ithaca, NY: Cornell University Press, 2006.

Valenzuela, Abel. "Regulating Day Labor: Worker Centers and Organizing in the Informal Economy." In *The Informal American City: Beyond Taco Trucks and Day Labor,* edited by Vinit Mukhija, Anastasia Loukaitou-Sideris, 261-76. Cambridge, MA: MIT Press, 2014.

Venkatesh, Sudhir Alladi. *American Project: The Rise and Fall of a Modern Ghetto.* Cambridge, MA: Harvard University Press, 2000.

———. *Off the Books: The Underground Economy of the Urban Poor.* Cambridge, MA: Harvard University Press, 2006.

Ward, Peter M. "The Reproduction of Informality in Low-Income Self-Help Housing Communities." In *The Informal American City: Beyond Taco Trucks and Day Labor,* edited by Vinit Mukhija, Anastasia Loukaitou-Sideris, 59-78. Cambridge, MA: MIT Press, 2014.

Watson, R. "Constitutive Practices and Garfinkel's Notion of Trust: Revisited." *Journal of Classical Sociology* 9, no. 4 (2009): 475-99.

Weber, L. R., and A. I. Carter. *The Social Construction of Trust.* New York: Springer, 2003.

Wherry, Frederick F. *The Culture of Markets.* Cambridge: Polity, 2012.

Wolch, Jennifer, and Michael Dear. *Malign Neglect: Homelessness in an American City.* San Francisco: Jossey-Bass, 1993.

Zukin, Sharon. *Naked City: The Death and Life of Authentic Urban Places.* Oxford: Oxford University Press, 2010.

Index

Adriana, 44
alcohol use: Alcoholics Anonymous, 120; and "bottoming
  out," 47, 96; Chuck's, 108-10;
  and distrust, 69; Jorge's, 44,
  72, 73; Raúl's, 114; Rennie's,
  44, 106-7, 109-10, 155, 161;
  Ricardo's, 100-102, 108; RJ's,
  112; Sal's, 95, 114; as social and
  symbolic act, 97-99, 101, 108;
  of visitors, 87, 88; and work, 3,
  4, 33, 86, 93, 96, 100-101, 120,
  121, 155. *See also* substance use
Alston, 133, 134
Andrea, 52, 53, 63, 90, 111
Ángel, 44
Anthony, 31, 60, 120
artwork, sale of, 3, 130-31, 140, 149
Avery, Jacob, 96, 156

Barbara, 52, 90
Beat generation, 17-18, 134, 139
Benson, 86-87, 102-5, 108, 116-18,
  157, 169
Betty, 167

blocks: as communities, 83, 92,
  154; in isolation from one
  another, 68; Kevin on, 83-84;
  Khaled on, 61-62, 65, 111;
  management of space on, 111;
  organization of, 79-80, 84;
  ownership of space on, 58-64;
  primacy of, 65, 83; profitable,
  143; stabilizing boardwalk, 63;
  symbolic presence on, 82
boardwalk: alcohol and drug use
  on, 95-97, 100, 108-10, 111,
  113, 155; available spaces on,
  86; Benson's work on, 103-5,
  117-19; blocks stabilizing, 63;
  "commercial" side as antithetical to boardwalk culture,
  142; community of workers
  on, 65, 139; configurations
  of precarity on, 14, 45, 153;
  constant flux on, 87; and
  dependence on web of people,
  83; description of, 1; dynamics of, 90-91, 93; economic
  activity on, 114, 116; economic

Doug/Vince, 88
"drama," 90-91, 93
drug dependency, 69, 113
drug economy, 10
drug trade, 22-23
drug use: Benson's, 104-5; on
    boardwalk, 86-87, 96, 99, 101;
    and "bottoming out," 47; as
    "disorder," 20; economic and
    social world of, 93; Khaled's,
    102, 107, 110; of marginalized
    groups, 33; problematic, 107; in
    public spaces, 97-98; symbolic
    role of, 97; tools for managing,
    8; and work, 96, 100, 108, 121,
    155. *See also* substance use
Duck, Waverly, 10
Duneier, Mitchell, 7, 21

economic activity, 21, 114
economic exchanges, 52, 123
economic landscape, 53
economic opportunities, 32
economic upheaval, 154
economic world, 116, 153
Electronic Benefits Transfer
    (EBT), 13, 135
Emilio, 47, 58, 63-64
Emma: on boardwalk, 67-68; com-
    munity service, 145; and land-
    lord, 30; moving residence,
    90; and social services, 2-3,
    12-13; son, 91, 102; weighing
    options, 8
Enrique, 102
ethnography, 25-31
expectations: for boardwalk, 6; in
    community of workers, 60, 73,
    74-76, 77-83, 88-89, 92

Farid, 59-60
Food Not Bombs, 21

Fred, 158-60
Free Speech Zone: boardwalk as,
    21, 167; boundaries between
    public and private spaces
    blurred, 139; economic oppor-
    tunities in, 69; permissible
    activities and merchandise in,
    34; regulation of, 37-39; and
    right to work, 156; sale of jew-
    elry banned from, 89; as space
    for political and ideological
    messaging, 133

General Relief funds, 4, 12, 135
gentrification, 24, 145
Gerald, 49
Gerry, Frank, 23
Google, 23-24, 142
Gowan, Teresa, 120

Harold, 110, 157, 165, 166
Hart, Keith, 10
Hazel, 42, 58-59, 90, 130-31, 140,
    141
homelessness: and bohemian
    identity, 109; crisis, 20; ex-
    periencing, 8, 33, 96, 121-22,
    167; increasing, 23, 24; and
    legitimacy, 154; literature on,
    118; and permit program, 44;
    policing, 4; problematic, 107;
    as social problem, 161, 166; as
    town hall topic, 57; vehicular,
    21; in Venice, 42
homeless people: communicating
    with, 91; in community of
    workers, 69, 116; population of,
    21, 43, 113; on Skid Row, 25

immigrants: economic precari-
    ousness of, 5-6; and economic
    trends, 19; lamenting long-

Tabor, Irving, 16
talent, 8, 50, 141, 156
tech industry, 15, 23, 142
Temporary Assistance for Needy Families (TANF), 4, 12, 122, 160
Tim: and Alston, 133–34; on Anthony's death, 120; and collective reappropriation of public space, 154; on donations, 135; feather earrings, 143; identity, 116; and lottery, 42–44; partnership with RJ, 59, 113, 132; purchasing merchandise, 145; on racialized impact of regulation, 137; as relatively privileged, 169–70; role for unhoused folks, 167; space usage, 60–63
Tiny, 110
Tom, 53
Tracy, 53
trust, 32, 68–69, 73, 82, 92–93
Tully, 35, 49

Umar, 169; and balance between cost of living and work options, 158–60; breaking down marketplace, 168; and durability of products, 127; enforcing substance control, 111, 156; and expectations, 82; Leia granting informal sick leave to, 81; making change for customer, 74–75, 76; and performative character of marketplace, 140; profit metrics, 142–43, 144; salvaging broken merchandise, 129–30; sleeping in car, 157

Venice: alcohol and drug use in, 99; annexation of, 15; antiwar and feminist movement in, 18; author's life in, 25–26; beach vibe of, 143; chaotic buzz of, 54; counterculture of, 107, 139; differing social positions in, 29; as Dogtown, 179n61; economy of, 16, 28; as European simulacrum, 1; Hazel in, 131; history of, 14, 17, 21, 25; homelessness in, 24, 42, 180n86; Julian in, 41; and lottery, 56; and municipal code, 37; public expressionists in, 138; regulation of, 57; vs. Santa Monica, 146; as studio, 140; tech industry in, 23–24; vendors in, 55–56; violence in, 22
Venkatesh, Sudhir Alladi, 98
violence: distinguished from subversive safety net, 13; as patterned response, 178n47; racial, 22–23; and substance use, 97; threats of, 90; in Venice, 22
vulnerability, 13, 71–72, 157

wage labor, 2–3, 10–11, 12, 19, 121, 155, 158, 160, 164–65, 178n46
Wes, 54
William, 137–38, 156

Zelda, 77
Zephyr, 115

www.ingramcontent.com/pod-product-compliance
Lightning Source LLC
Chambersburg PA
CBHW032136020426
42334CB00016B/1188